THE LABRADOR RETRIEVER

Diane Morgan

The Labrador Retriever

Project Team
Editor: Stephanie Fornino
Copy Editor: Carl Schutt
Design: Tilly Grassa
Series Design: Mada Design
Series Originator: Dominique De Vito

T.F.H. Publications
President/CEO: Glen S. Axelrod
Executive Vice President: Mark E. Johnson
Publisher: Christopher T. Reggio
Production Manager: Kathy Bontz

T.F.H. Publications, Inc.
One TFH Plaza
Third and Union Avenues
Neptune City, NJ 07753

ISBN 978-0-7938-3636-9

Printed and bound in China.
08 09 10   7 9 8

Library of Congress Cataloging-in-Publication Data Morgan, Diane, 1947- The labrador retriever / Diane Morgan.
p. cm.
Includes index.
ISBN 0-7938-3636-0 (alk. paper)
1.   Labrador retriever. I. Title.
SF429.L3M666 2005
636.752'7--dc22
2005006545

This book has been published with the intent to provide accurate and authoritative information in regard to the subject matter within. While every reasonable precaution has been taken in preparation of this book, the author and publisher expressly disclaim responsibility for any errors, omissions, or adverse effects arising from the use or application of the information contained herein. The techniques and suggestions are used at the reader's discretion and are not to be considered a substitute for veterinary care. If you suspect a medical problem consult your veterinarian.

The Leader In Responsible Animal Care For Over 50 Years!®
www.tfh.com

TABLE OF CONTENTS

HISTORY
of the Labrador Retriever

Welcome to the world of the Labrador Retriever! Although the Labrador's origins lie in the chilly wastes of Canada, today this remarkable dog warms the hearts of everyone who touches—or is touched—by him. Superior water dog, hunter, obedience dog, and pet, the Labrador is a treasured friend and companion.

THE LABRADOR IN NEWFOUNDLAND

While it's only natural to assume that Labrador Retrievers came from Labrador, it turns out that Newfoundland is entitled to the honor. Admittedly, the connection between Newfoundland and Labrador is a bit obscure, although both are part of the same Canadian province now called "Newfoundland and Labrador," presumably to make things less confusing.

The Origin of Newfoundland

Newfoundland is an amazing place. Lying open along a major storm track, it is vulnerable to the gales and rages, including winter cyclones, of the rough North Atlantic Ocean. No place on the island is more than approximately 62 miles from the sea. In fact, Newfoundland has been documented as one of the foggiest, snowiest, wettest, cloudiest, and windiest inhabited places on the planet. It's cold, too, with the glacial Labrador Current holding July average temperatures in coastal areas to around 57°F. Inland temperatures may climb to the dizzying heights of about 61°F. It may sound awful, but Newfoundlanders are actually quite proud of their climate. They claim it's invigorating and character building. Perhaps it is, because the Labrador is certainly one of the hardiest and noblest of all dogs.

Newfoundland is currently in Canada, although it wasn't always that way. Originally, Newfoundland was its own separate British colony. It was "discovered" in 1494 by some European fishermen and traders from the Bristol Company. However surprised *they* may have been to run into the place, Newfoundland had been found first by the Dorset Eskimo people, who had been living there for centuries.

How the Lab Got His Name

Many authorities trace the origin of the name "Labrador" to João Fernandes, a Portuguese explorer, and "llavrador," or "land holder," from the Azores. Originally, the name Labrador was applied to what was then thought to be a continuous stretch of land from Greenland to Newfoundland. Later, when it became obvious that Greenland was separated from the Canadian coast by Baffin Bay and the Davis Strait, the name Labrador was used to designate the neighboring mainland coast.

By one way of reckoning, Labrador is part of Newfoundland, so calling the breed the Labrador Retriever isn't that far off the mark after all. Labrador is just northwest off the island of Newfoundland. Geographically, the province consists of the island of Newfoundland and the mainland Labrador. In 1949, Labrador and Newfoundland joined in a confederation, and Newfoundlanders became Canadian citizens. Since 1964, the province has referred to itself at a provincial level as "Newfoundland and Labrador," but federally the name "Newfoundland" alone was used. However, in 2001, a constitutional amendment was passed by the Senate, the House of Commons, and the House of Assembly changing the official name to "Newfoundland and Labrador."

Early Labradors in Newfoundland

At any rate, the earliest note of Labradors was made in 1822, when a visitor to Newfoundland mentioned these black, sleek-coated water retrievers. Unlike most other retrievers of the day, these dogs had short, oily, heavy coats that shed water. Exactly what breeds originally went into making the Labrador is a mystery, however. At one time it was believed that the Labrador was a scaled-down offshoot of the large, furry Newfoundland dog. The theory was that there were two related breeds, the Greater Newfoundland and the Lesser Newfoundland, alternately known as the Greater and Lesser St. John's dogs. The larger, heavily coated dog was used mostly as a draft animal for hauling fish around. The smaller breed was smooth coated and renowned for his stamina. This breed, ancestor of the present-day Labrador, was designed as a fishing/retrieving breed, a function that it filled admirably.

According to this theory, the early "Labradors" (or small Newfies) were used to help haul in fishing lines and retrieve fish that fell off hooks. What was needed was a dog small enough to fit in a small boat but strong enough to help haul in nets. The dogs therefore needed a dense, oily coat that would retain heat and repel ice, as well as a willing-to-please personality and a tough work ethic. It is said that after working all day, these dogs would come home to play with the fishermen's children in the evening. This theory has fallen out of favor recently, although it can't actually be disproved. Whether or not Labs are really descended from Newfies may never been known unless some elaborate DNA testing will reveal the secrets of their genes. It is not even known whether these dogs were a native breed or whether they were brought over from Europe by some long-forgotten settlers. The two main Native American tribes of the area, the Dorset Eskimos and the Beothuck Indians, left no mention of dog breeding or dogs at all, in fact. That doesn't mean they didn't breed them, however. It just means they never happened to mention it!

The earliest European settlers (16th century) to the area mostly hailed from Devon, England. They were renowned for their hunting and outdoors skills, which were very necessary if you were thinking about tramping around Newfoundland in the winter. Because of these skills, some dog historians surmise that these settlers may have brought their black St. Hubert's Hounds (a breed which figures in the development of many other breeds, including the Basset Hound) with them. These dogs were probably crossbred with other dogs, either native or imported, until something approximating the present Labrador appeared. It is very likely that the original Newfoundland dog, the French St. Hubert's Hound, and various native breeds all participated in the development of the present-day Lab. A great majority of these early "Labradors" were black, although a yellow or even a chocolate occasionally made an appearance. These other colors were labeled differently depending on the observer and possibly the shade observed.

The Labrador Retriever is a noble and hardy breed.

Because the St. John's area of Newfoundland was the center of both the fishing industry and the dog who was part of it, the Labrador was first known as St. John's dog. Sadly, the original St. John's dog became extinct. As early as 1780, the law forbade more than one dog per family, apparently because of a concern over packs of dogs attacking sheep. Then, the Sheep

Lab Colors Through Time

Although black was the preferred color for Labrador Retrievers until quite recently, it should be noted that even the old-time St. John's dogs occasionally showed up as yellow or chocolate. In the beginning, puppies who featured these colors were culled from the litter until people eventually decided that these colors were desirable after all.

Protection Act of 1885 was passed. This imposed a heavy tax and license for owning a dog, especially a female. Thus, many female puppies were killed at birth. This was a big waste of life and money, by the way, because sheep farming never did catch on in Newfoundland. Another factor leading to the near extinction of the breed was that English quarantine laws forbade the importation of any more dogs due to the fear of rabies. (In fact, the quarantine was just lifted a few years ago.)

If the history of the Labrador seems confusing, don't despair! The confusion stems from the fact that we don't really know the details about the earliest Labradors. This has led to people simply trying to construct a theory that fits the known facts, which does make sense. However, it is quite possible that most of the theories regarding the origins of this great breed hold some truth.

Regardless of what the Lab came to be called, the breed was always known as a hardworking hunting dog.

THE LABRADOR IN ENGLAND

The Labrador is inextricably mixed up with the various English Earls of Malmesbury. The second Earl of Malmesbury (1778-1841) had these dogs imported to Heron (Hurn) Court, England, in about 1830. Apparently, while at the British seaport of Poole, he happened to see a pair who had been brought into the country from Newfoundland by various schooners and fishing boats. After observing the dogs happily catching sticks and abandoned fish for some small boys, he conjectured that these dogs might make excellent waterfowl retrievers. He called the dogs "Little Newfoundlers."

It was this earl who began the first actual kennel for Labradors, a hobby to which he devoted himself until his death. In fact, he and his son, the Third Earl of Malmesbury (1807-1889), bred the dogs from which most modern Labradors can trace their ancestry. The third earl was also the one who gave the dog the name he bears today rather than "Little Newfoundler" or "St. John's Retriever." Perhaps the earl had something against St. John; perhaps he just liked Labrador. It's hard to tell at this juncture.

Other early breeders included the fifth Duke of Buccleuch (1806-1884) in Scotland. (His real name was Walter Francis Montagu Douglas Scott.) Buccleuch began his kennel independently of the second Earl of Malmesbury in about 1835. Buccleuch's brother, John Scott, was also an early breeder, as was the tenth Earl of Home. Their families stayed involved with the breed for generations.

The Second Earl of Malmesbury became interested in Labradors after observing them catching sticks and abandoned fish for some children.

The entire breed would most likely have died out if it wasn't for a chance meeting between the three noblemen who had taken such a fancy to it. The story goes that the sixth Duke of Buccleuch (1831-1914) and the twelfth Duke of Home (1834-1918) were visiting a sick aunt. They also ran into the old third Earl of Malmesbury along the way. At any rate, the three of them decided to get together for a waterfowl shoot on the southern

For some reason, it seems that no matter what you cross a Labrador with, the Labrador genes seem to dominate those of the other breed. In other words, cross anything with a Lab and the offspring will look more like a Lab than anything else. I know from personal experience that if you cross a Lab with a Basset Hound, you will get a Lab on very short legs!

coast. Apparently, Home and Buccleuch were so impressed by Malmesbury's dogs that their interest in the breed was renewed. Malmesbury, contrary to the common practice of the time, had kept his line very pure by continuing to import from Newfoundland. At that time, most breeders "outcrossed" regularly with other breeds, probably as an experiment. However, only a purebred Lab retained all the great qualities the early breeders wanted, and Malmesbury had those dogs. He gave a few of his dogs to the other two men so that the three could carry on the breeding program, and the rest is history! Happily, the Buccleuch Kennel still exists, maintaining its pure Labrador lines.

The sixth Earl of Malmesbury referred to his dogs in a letter as "Labrador" retrievers, and the name has stuck ever since. He wrote, "We always call mine Labrador dogs and I have kept the breed as pure as I could from the first I had from Poole....[the breed has] a close coat which turns the water off like oil and, above all, a tail like an otter." That otter tail remains part of the breed standard even today.

In 1892, the sixth Duke of Buccleuch was pleased to announce the birth of two liver-colored puppies. It is assumed that the liver-colored dogs were what is now referred to as "chocolate," but this term wasn't applied until the late 1930s in two British kennels.

The English took the Labradors they did have and began cross-breeding with other retrievers, at least for a while. In 1903, the Kennel Club recognized the Labrador as a separate breed, and further cross-breeding ceased. The British royal family was highly interested in Labradors, and their patronage helped get the Labrador started off on the right paw, so to speak. In 1916, the first Labrador Club was established in England by Lord Knutsford (Munden Kennels) and Lady Lorna, Countess of Howe (Banchory Labradors). One of her black dogs, Dual Champion Banchory Bolo (1915-1927), had some white hair under the pads of his feet. These white hairs can be seen today in many of his descendants and are called "Bolo pads" in his honor.

THE LABRADOR IN NORTH AMERICA

Labradors were imported into the United States before World War I, but they were initially grouped along with other retrievers as a single breed. The American Kennel Club recognized the breed as separate in 1917, but ten years later only 23 retrievers of *all* kinds (Labs, Flat-Coated, Golden, Curly-Coated, and Chesapeake) were registered. It is commonly stated that the first Labrador Retriever registered with the AKC was a Scottish bitch named Brocklehirst

Other Lab Names

Over the years, Labradors and their near relations have been known by many names, including: St. John's Dog, Lesser St. John's Dog, Newfoundland Dog, Lesser Newfoundland Dog, Little Newfoundlanders, Newfoundland Water Dog, Labrador Dog, St. John's Labrador Dog, Black Water Dog, Lesser Labrador, Smaller Labrador, English Retriever, and English Labrador.

The term "chocolate" to describe a Lab's color was not used in England until the late 1930s.

The American Kennel Club (AKC), founded in 1884, is the most influential dog club in the United States. The AKC is a "club of clubs," meaning that its members are other kennel clubs, not individual people. The AKC registers purebred dogs, supervises dog shows, and is concerned with all dog-related matters, including public education and legislation. It collects and publishes the official standards for all of its recognized breeds.

The United Kingdom version of the AKC is called the Kennel Club. However, the Kennel Club's members are individual persons. The membership of the Kennel Club is restricted to a maximum of 1,500 UK members in addition to 50 overseas members and a small number of honorary life members. The Kennel Club promotes responsible dog ownership and works on important issues like canine health and welfare.

Floss in 1917. However, further study has revealed that Labradors named Virginia Vennie and Virginia Myra were registered in 1914. (Part of the confusion stems from the fact that back in 1914, Labs were not recognized by the AKC as a separate breed.) However, the Lab didn't begin his inexorable rise to popularity until the early 1930s.

Snobbery played an unexpectedly important role in bringing the Labrador to the United States. Scottish "pass shooting" styles became the rage, and status-seeking wealthy people bought their guns from the best London gunsmiths and their dogs from British and Scottish kennels. These people turned their estates into vast private hunting preserves. They also imported young Scottish gamekeepers and organized "shoots" like the ones held in Europe. These shoots were the ancestors of today's field trials.

On October 7, 1931 the Labrador Retriever Club was established in the United States, and the first American field trial for Labradors was held at Glenmere Court Estate in Chester, New York on December 21, 1931. The motivating force behind both the Club and the trials was a man named Franklin B. Lord. The goals of the Club were stated as follows:

(a) To maintain, foster and encourage a spirit of cooperation in the breeding, owning and exhibiting of pure bred Labrador Retriever dogs by individuals, organizations, kennel clubs, show clubs and specialty clubs

(b) To formulate, define, ascertain and publish the standard type of Labrador Retriever dogs and to procure standard type of Labrador Retriever dogs and to induce the adoption of said standard type by breeders, judges, dog owners, dog show committees and others, and to endeavor to have standard type recognized by all, so that the Labrador Retriever breed shall be judged by said standard.

(c) To encourage foster help, aid and assistance to protect and increase the interest of people in the Labrador dog breed.

(d) To offer prizes, create publicity and give and support shows where Labrador Retriever dogs are exhibited.

(e) To do all such acts and things as are incident or conducive to the premises and generally to do all acts and things and to exercise all the powers now or hereafter authorized by law necessary to carry on the said Corporation or to promote any of the objects of said Corporation, all of which shall be conducted without pecuniary profits.

On May 18, 1933, the first American specialty show for Labradors was held in New York City. Best in Show was awarded to a dog named Boli of Blake, owned by none other than Franklin B. Lord, founder of the Labrador Retriever Club. Boli was the first Labrador to earn an American championship. The show was judged by Mrs. Marshall Field, of department store fame. In 1938, a black Labrador owned by W. Averill Harriman was the first dog to appear on the cover of *Life* magazine. He won the top retriever stake at four years of age. Another Lab, King Buck, was the first to appear on a United States postage stamp in 1959.

In 1991, Labrador Retrievers jumped into first place in AKC registrations, a position the breed holds up to the present time, and with reason. Hunter, show dog, field trialer, agility dog, obedience dog, and best of all, family pet—the Labrador Retriever is truly America's Dog!

The Practically Perfect Lab

The first Labrador to win Best in Show at an all-breed show was Champion Earlsmoor Moor of Arden, born February 1, 1937 and owned by Mr. and Mrs. Samuel Milbank. He was shown 42 times. Of those he won Best of Breed 40 times, placed in the Sporting Group 27 times, won the Sporting Group 12 times, was awarded Best in Show 5 times, and won the National Specialty 5 times. This top conformation dog also ran and placed in field trials. A wonderful portrait of this great dog, Standing Black Labrador, painted by Reuben Ward Binks, is currently on display at the AKC Museum of the Dog in St. Louis, Missouri. The portrait is said to display the perfect Labrador in every respect.

The Labrador is a versatile dog who excels at a variety of activities.

13

CHARACTERISTICS
of the Labrador Retriever

I n the United States alone, more than 100,000 new Labrador Retrievers are registered with the American Kennel Club every year, making this the most popular breed in America. It is also the most popular breed in the United Kingdom and Australia.

LOOKING AT LABRADORS

To discover the ideal overall picture of the Labrador, the first place to look is the breed standard. While the standard can be interpreted in various ways by different people and can even change over the years, it still represents the "perfect" dog. The present American Kennel Club breed standard was approved February 12, 1994 and became effective March 31, 1994. The present Kennel Club breed standard went into effect in September 2000.

According to the breed standards, Labradors are well balanced and strongly built. Their distinguishing features include their short, dense, weather-resistant coat, otter tail, clean-cut head, and kind eyes (that match their kind hearts). The life expectancy of the Labrador is 10 to 12 years, but many make it well into their teens if given good care and a proper diet.

The following description of the Labrador Retriever is based on interpretations of both the American Kennel Club and Kennel Club's breed standards.

Color

Labradors come in three solid colors: black, yellow, and chocolate. A small white spot on the chest is permissible but not desirable.

Does color indicate temperament? Many people swear that of the three colors, the yellows are the sweetest and calmest and chocolates are the wildest. There haven't been any DNA studies linking color and temperament, but there has been enough anecdotal evidence on this score to suggest that it's possible. If there is indeed any truth to a relationship between different colors and different temperaments, the reason is probably not that there's an actual genetic linkage between color and temperament but because present-day

The Labrador is a well-balanced, strongly built dog.

chocolates share a similar lineage. In other words, the first chocolate Labs may have been dogs with exceptionally bouncy spirits in a chocolate-colored coat, and the offspring inherited both. There are plenty of highly excitable yellow Labs and plenty of sedate chocolate Labs, of course, so even if there is a genetic link, it's a pretty fragile one.

Some people believe that black Labradors have fewer health and personality disorders than their chocolate and yellow counterparts. No scientific evidence supports this, but the suggestion is that the gene pool is larger for black Labs.

Body Type

According to the American Kennel Club, the height at the withers or shoulders for an adult male is 22.5 to 24.4 inches, while for a female it is 21.5 to 23.5 inches. Any variation of more than half an inch above or below those heights will disqualify a dog in the show ring, although of course he or she can still make a terrific pet! The approximate ideal weight for males in good working condition is 65 to 80 pounds, while for females it is 55 to 70 pounds. However, I have seen large males who tipped the scales at over 100 pounds.

The Kennel Club maintains that the ideal height for a Labrador at the withers is 22 to 22.5 inches for males and 21.5 to 22 inches for females.

The ideal Labrador is short-coupled, with well-sprung ribs. The body should be long enough to permit a straight, efficient stride, but the dog should never appear low and long or tall and leggy in outline. Dogs who are "light" or "weedy" or "cloddy" or "lumbering" are incorrect.

Head

The skull should be wide and well developed with a moderate stop (where the muzzle meets the skull). The lips should fall away in a curve toward the throat. Black and yellow Labs should have black noses, and chocolate Labs should have brown noses. A pink or unpigmented nose is a disqualification in the show ring. The nose should be wide and the nostrils well developed.

The ideal dog has a scissors bite, with the upper teeth overlapping the lower ones. A level bite is acceptable but not desirable. Overshot or undershot jaws are serious faults, as are missing molars.

The eyes should be brown in black and yellow Labradors and brown or hazel in chocolate Labradors. The eye rims should be black in black and yellow Labradors and brown in chocolate Labradors. Eye rims lacking pigmentation are disqualifying faults. Black or yellow eyes are undesirable, as are round, prominent eyes, small eyes set close together, or any kind of eye that gives a harsh expression to the dog.

Neck

The neck should rise strongly from the shoulders with a moderate arch. A short, thick neck or a "ewe" neck is incorrect, because the neck should be of the proper length to reach the ground to retrieve game. (I haven't actually seen any dogs of any breed who couldn't reach the ground with their mouths, but perhaps this is quibbling.) The back should be strong, with a level topline from the withers to the croup when standing or moving. The chest should be *moderately* wide, neither narrow nor barrel-chested. The underline is almost straight, with little or no tuck-up in mature dogs.

Forequarters and Hindquarters

Some people believe that black Labradors may have fewer health and personality disorders than their chocolate and yellow counterparts.

The forequarters should be muscular and balanced, with sloping shoulders that form an angle of about 90 degrees with the upper arm. Straight or overmuscled shoulders are penalized. In the ideal dog, the length of the shoulder blade should equal the length of the upper arm. When viewed from the front, the legs should be straight with good, strong bone. Viewed from the side, the elbows should be directly under the withers, and the front legs should be perpendicular to the ground and well under the body. The elbows should be close to the ribs without looseness. The feet are strong and compact, with well-arched toes and well-developed pads. Dewclaws may be removed. Dogs with a long back and short legs are penalized.

The Labrador's hindquarters are broad, muscular, and well developed. Viewed from the rear, the hind legs are straight and parallel. Viewed from the side, the angulation of the rear legs is in balance with the front. The angulation of both stifle and hock joint is such as to achieve the optimal balance of drive and traction. When standing, the rear toes are only slightly behind the point of the rump. The feet are strong and compact, with well-arched toes and well-developed pads.

Fédération Cynologique Internationale

While many people have only heard of the American Kennel Club, Kennel Club, and perhaps some other national kennel clubs, an international organization actually exists. The Fédération Cynologique Internationale is the World Canine Organization, which includes 80 members and contract partners (one member per country), each of which issues its own pedigrees and trains its own judges. The founding nations were Germany, Austria, Belgium, France, and the Netherlands. It was first formed in 1911 but later disappeared during World War I. The organization was reconstituted in 1921. Currently, neither the United States nor Canada is a member.

The FCI ensures that its pedigrees and judges are recognized by all FCI members. Every member country conducts international shows as well as working trials; results are sent to the FCI office, where they are input into computers. When a dog has been awarded a certain number of awards, he can receive the title of International Beauty or Working Champion. These titles are confirmed by the FCI. The FCI recognizes 331 dog breeds, and each of them is the "property" of a specific country, ideally the one in which the breed developed. The owner countries of the breeds write the standard of these breeds in cooperation with the Standards and Scientific Commissions of the FCI, and the translation and updating are carried out by the FCI. In addition, via the national canine organization and the FCI, every breeder can ask for international protection of his or her kennel name.

Tail

The tail is very important in Labradors! It is no mere appendage but a device to help steer the dog through icy waters. The breed standards are very explicit about the tail. Labrador owners often joke that the tail is carried exactly at coffee table height. Docking is not permitted.

Coat

The coat is such a traditional part of the Labrador look that its description has not changed in the American Kennel Club breed standard for more than 60 years. The coat should be short, straight, and very dense, feeling fairly hard to the touch. There should also be a soft, downy, weather-resistant undercoat that provides protection from water, cold, and thickets. The outer coat is hard and water repellant. A slight wave down the back is permissible, but a woolly coat is not. A heavy coat that "stands off" from the skin is also not permissible.

Movement

The movement of the Labrador should be free and effortless. When watching a dog move toward you in a straight line without pacing or weaving, the legs should form straight lines. When viewing the dog from the rear, the hind legs should move as closely as possible in a parallel line with the front legs. When viewed from the side, the shoulders should move freely and effortlessly. The Lab's webbed feet make him a great swimmer.

Temperament

The legendary stable temperament of the Labrador is part of the breed standards. One of the earliest dog writers, a man who went by the nickname of Stonehenge, wrote of the Lab back in 1873: "The evidences of a good temper must be regarded with great care since his utility depends on his disposition."

People who love Labs (and who doesn't?) choose the breed primarily for its trainability and *joie de vivre*. If you long for a dog with energy to spare, an enthusiastic outlook, and a happy demeanor, the Labrador may be just right for you. If you have multiple enemies, the Lab is not a reliable protector. However, if you have lots of friends, your Lab will be eager to share them with you. They are definitely people-oriented dogs.

According to the AKC breed standard, the Lab's coat should be short, straight, and very dense, with a weather-resistant undercoat.

VARIATIONS ON THE STANDARD

Conformation Versus Working Labs

Although the breed standard is meant to apply to both conformation (show or bench) dogs and working field dogs, there has been a recent trend toward the development of two different types of Labradors: a working type and a showing type. It has been said that field dogs are athletes and bench dogs are models, the first type being bred for hunting ability and the second for show and temperament. (Pet Labradors might be of either "type," depending on the line the dog came from.) Many other breeds in the Sporting Group demonstrate the same tendency. The "problem," if there is one, lies squarely in the court of the conformation set, who depend on the subjective opinion of judges as to what the best example of the breed is. In field trials and in real hunting conditions, performance is what counts. I am not persuaded, however, that there's anything necessarily "wrong" with having two different types within a breed. There are two types of dogs because there are two types of owners with two different objectives.

Physical Types

Bench people sometimes complain that field people are breeding dogs who don't look like Labs and who don't have the correct temperament, while field people assert that conformation Labradors have lost most of their hunting ability. The truth is that many bench-type dogs are adequate hunters, and many field trial dogs have superb (although exuberant) temperaments. But the difference is real, and it's something a buyer may wish to take into consideration before purchasing a Labrador Retriever.

For whatever reason, Labradors do seem to come in distinct physical types (referred to by various names). The shape of the head, the set of the tail, and the texture of the coat vary somewhat among the various types. This "typing" is not an official designation, and descriptions depend on who is making the divisions among the types. Such designations include "upland Labs," "water Labs," "American Labs," and "English Labs." While there are subtle differences among all of these, in general, "field," "upland," and "American" types are taller, longer in the body, and lighter boned than their "show," "water," or "English"

Water Wonders

Of all retrievers, Labradors are the fastest swimmers, easily outpacing Chesapeake Bay Retrievers and Golden Retrievers in the water.

Of all retrievers, Labradors are the fastest swimmers.

counterparts. Many also agree that the so-called English type is calmer and more laid back, as well as stockier, wider, and smaller than the American type. English Labs tend toward obesity. This type also may have a greater tendency toward developing a mild form of hip dysplasia, because they generally have some hip joint subluxation. Epilepsy, too, seems more common in the English lines, although again, it's generally a rather mild form.

The New England Lab

One offshoot of the English Lab is the unofficially titled "New England Labrador." These animals are even shorter than the English form but have less bone and a less pronounced head. They are generally smaller than the official standard for the breed. Their legs are very short, a feature selected for by generations of waterfowl hunters who needed a very compact dog who could be easily hauled into a boat from the water. The energy level of the New England Labrador is somewhere between the English and American types; they have to have a higher energy level than show dogs, but they need to be calm enough to remain quiet in a boat.

The American Field Lab

This type of Labrador is the complete opposite of the New England Lab. American field Labs are taller, rangier, and designed for upland field work more so than for water work. They may be more "snipey" in the face. These Labs also have a much higher energy level than the New England version. These are tough dogs who require experienced trainers to bring out their best in demanding field work.

CHARACTERISTICS OF THE LABRADOR

Labradors belong to the Sporting Group in the American Kennel Club designation and to the Gundog Group according to the Kennel Club. The Labrador's job is to flush birds and retrieve them, and Labs can work both upland game and waterfowl. They will even break ice to dive and get the bird. Recently, some Labrador strains have shown some pointing ability as well.

Unlike some other breeds, the Labrador is an excellent choice for the responsible first-time dog owner. In fact, the Lab may spoil you

The Labrador is proficient at flushing and retrieving birds, and he can work upland game and fowl.

for other breeds! These are happy, friendly, adaptable, intelligent, and optimistic dogs. They thrive on love, are easily bored, and enjoy life most if they are given something interesting to do. In fact, the Labrador is one of the main breeds used for guide and rescue.

You can make a good argument that Labradors are, all things considered, the very best family dogs. They excel at most events in the dog world and love swimming, playing, or just hanging around with you. They are great with children and other pets and are gentle with the elderly and disabled. In addition, they are smart, athletic, loyal, and trainable. Many people agree that this is one of the most intelligent dog breeds.

All Labradors need regular and vigorous exercise or they can become bored and destructive.

Adaptability

Labs are known as being rather "insensitive" dogs in the best possible meaning of the term. It takes a lot to perturb a Labrador, and they put up with moving, strange company, screaming kids, and other household upsets. Even Labradors who have been abused by their previous owners seem to bounce back with remarkable good cheer once placed in a loving family.

Labradors don't like being left alone for long periods, however. Remember, this is a breed that was developed for working in close contact with human beings for long hours every day. They expect to do so. When feeling bored or neglected, they can become destructive or develop habits like monotonous barking. This behavior is merely a plea for help from a highly intelligent and social being. When given proper attention and care, though, most Labs are extremely laid back and quiet around the house: that is, after they pass their boisterous puppyhood stage!

Labrador Retrievers generally get along very well with other dogs. They are peaceable animals who enjoy playing and interacting with other dogs. They also get along very well with cats and other pets. Of course, proper socialization and early training are important factors in making a multi-pet household a success.

Eating Habits

Labs eat everything. Many Labradors excel in the food-stealing department, and you always have to be careful to keep leftovers out of their reach. They gain weight easily, too. What they don't eat, they may chew. The Lab is a very mouthy dog who needs to be supervised carefully, especially when he's young.

Exercise Requirements

All Labradors, even the calmest, need regular and vigorous exercise. If they don't get it, they can become bored and destructive. Young dogs in particular are very exuberant, and they can easily knock over a child. You can keep a Labrador in an apartment if you are vigilant about sufficient exercise.

Guarding Ability

While Labradors love their families and are incredibly loyal, most of them will not attack an intruder. Some will bark in a threatening way, but that's usually as far as it goes—or needs to, for that matter! A large barking dog will usually scare intruders into leaving. If not, the intruder is likely to be licked to death by the happy Labrador.

Health Problems

Because of their surge in popularity, Labradors from less-than-reliable sources may be host to numerous health problems. In fact, due to overbreeding, there has been a large increase in physical and psychological problems now showing up in the breed that were never there before. Hip dysplasia, peripheral retinal atrophy, retinal dysplasia, and even aggression are now appearing in Labradors, a breed once renowned for its soundness and good temperament. Fortunately, you can avoid much of the heartache of owning such a dog by doing your research beforehand and purchasing your dog from a trustworthy source.

Hunting

Labradors, developed as hunting dogs in the English environment, possess the characteristics needed to work very closely with the hunter, including a desire to stick close but fetch game when commanded. (Pointers and setters hunt more independently, as they are expected to point out the birds first.) One of the great gifts of the Labrador, however, is that he has adapted well to upland game hunting as well as water retrieval work. Some hunters view the Labrador as replacing two dogs: spaniels for flushing upland game and Chesapeake Bay Retrievers for finding game in the water. Recently, some breeders have also worked at improving the pointing ability of Labrador Retrievers. If they accomplish this, they will indeed have developed an all-purpose hunting dog who can do three major hunting tasks: pointing, flushing, and retrieving! Even more amazing, they can perform these tasks on land or water.

Highly trainable, the Lab responds well to rewards like food, toys, play, and praise.

Shedding

Labradors shed more than you might think. They are not really a "short-haired" breed but a medium-coated breed with a very heavy double coat. They also shed year round, not just in the spring and fall. Regular brushing and the use of a shedding blade will reduce but not eliminate this normal process.

Temperament

The Labrador has an excellent disposition and is wonderful with children. However, this is a very active, powerful dog who needs plenty of exercise to help him burn calories and work off some of his energy. He will alert his family at the approach of visitors, but Labs are not protective. They'll greet everyone (even your mother-in-law) with joyful abandon. The Lab is known for his quick intellect, too, but give him time to develop. This breed is slow to mature.

Trainability

Labs are highly trainable, and they respond almost equally well to the three kinds of rewards: food, toys/play, and praise. However, they do need to be trained or they can get out of control easily. They also require early leash work. These powerful dogs can be pullers of the first order! Labradors are eager-to-please dogs, so all they really need is careful, consistent training to excel at a variety of endeavors.

LABRADOR SENSES

Sight

Humans and dogs see things differently. People are better at depth perception, color perception, and detecting minute details. Dogs, however, surpass humans in their ability to see at night. They are also quicker to respond to images and can detect motion better.

Smell

With their super-sensitive noses, dogs can collect all kinds of valuable information. Dogs have an olfactory region about 14 times larger than that of humans, and their smelling ability is much more advanced. There's no big mystery about this. Dogs have bigger noses, with a much larger area of olfactory mucous membranes containing many more smell receptors.

When dogs sniff the urine or anal sac region of other dogs, they learn about that animal's sexual status, social position, age, and even health. Other parts of the body contain some of the same information, but it's more intense in the anal region. Don't discourage your pet from using this time-honored greeting with other dogs; it's part of the normal socialization process.

Dogs possess a vomeronasal organ, a paired structure lying in the nasal septum that detects pheromones. Each vomeronasal organ opens into the incisive duct, the passage that connects the oral and nasal passages. It helps dogs recognize their relatives and directs their sexual behavior.

Hearing

Dogs also usually outperform human beings in the hearing department. They can hear higher-pitched sounds than we can, hence the famous dog whistle. It is important for dogs to be able hear these high-pitched sounds, because many rodents squeak in this range. Dogs have an uncanny ability to suddenly start digging like mad in the ground to extract a mole or small rodent.

In addition to their ability to hear higher sounds, dogs can also detect fainter sounds and pinpoint them more accurately. J.A.

The Nose Knows

Dogs have a far greater sense of smell than do humans, which is why they successfully sniff out everything from missing people to dangerous substances. It is also why they enjoy when their humans cook—so many delicious smells!

Altman at the Pavlov Institute of Physiology found that dogs can accurately locate the source of a sound in six hundredths of a second. The ability to pinpoint sounds is partly due to the cup shape of the ear, a basic form unaffected by whether the ears are erect or floppy.

Dogs can also move one ear at a time. Much of this mobility is due to the 16 muscles that control ear movement.

LABRADOR BODY LANGUAGE

Many dog signals are very subtle and sometimes appear mixed. If you are having trouble understanding a dog's signals, the safest thing to do is to assume the dog is aggressive or anxious, and *back off*.

Aggression

In the dog world, a stare is a challenge, sort of like a slap in the face. Most domestic dogs have learned that in our world, a stare from their owners might mean friendly attention, and most have learned to gaze back at us adoringly. But it's still a little against dog nature, and most dogs respond differently to stares from strangers than they do from their owners. It's more natural for dogs to glance away from us. A dominant or aggressive dog will stare back at us and perhaps growl. That's a danger signal. Other body language that may signal aggression includes ears laid back and close to the head, a tense body standing tall, lips open to expose the teeth, and a half-mast, horizontal, slowly wagging tail.

In general, confident, alert dogs stand tall with raised heads and erect, forward-pointing ears. Their eyes are wide and their mouths are closed or open only slightly. They will stare intently. They may wag their tails slowly at "half staff." If feeling aggressive or threatened, they may raise their hackles and growl. When meeting such a dog, it is best not to stare directly back, which the dog may regard as a threat. However, a cringing attitude on your part will give the dog the wrong impression, especially if he is your dog! The best plan is to gaze aloofly at the tip of the animal's ear. This shows that you are not threatening, but you are a grandiose creature too far above his limited ability to influence (even if this is not strictly true). However, a stiff-necked position on your part also constitutes threat, so be sure to bend it a little.

Fearfulness

Fearful dogs tend to lower their heads and tuck in their tails in an effort to appear smaller. They will avoid direct eye contact and in severe cases may "leak" urine. Other dog fear signals may include sniffing the ground (an appeasement sign), turning the head away or holding it to the side, or glancing quickly to the side. Fearful dogs should be treated similarly to aggressive ones, because fear can become aggression.

If you think a dog is fearful, approach slowly at an angle and look away from the dog. Fearful dogs, especially black ones, may also lick their noses. (The theory here is that a pink tongue against black fur is an especially visible sign.) Yawning is also a sign of a fearful, stressed dog. However, if you yawn back at your dog, especially an older dog who is used to you, it may serve to calm him down.

A friendly dog will tend to have an open, relaxed mouth and a relaxed but direct gaze.

Friendliness

Friendly dogs wag their tails gently or in an excited, happy way. They tend to have an open, relaxed mouth and may bark in short, excited "yips." When he wants to play, the friendly dog will "bow" down to engage you in some vigorous roughhousing. He will have a relaxed but direct gaze. His mouth will open in a grin.

Every dog is an individual, and it seems an injustice in a way to generalize. But if you take into account the basic qualities of the Labrador:

L = Loyalty
A = Affection
B = Bravery
R = Ruggedness
A = Agility
D = Determination
O = Obedience
R = Retriever

What more could you ask for?

PREPARING
for Your Labrador Retriever

Once you have made the decision that the Labrador is the breed for you, it's time to go about the exciting task of finding the right dog and preparing your home for him. However, you must remember that while the love of a Lab is free, the rest of him is not. Maintenance costs, which include things like food, grooming supplies, and veterinary care, can be expensive. The first year will be especially expensive, because you'll be buying a crate and other one-time purchases. Still, many people consider these expenses a small price to pay for owning the dog of their dreams.

FINDING A LABRADOR RETRIEVER

Everybody loves puppies, and nothing can be more cuddly and charming. It's also true that with a puppy you have a blank slate upon which to draw, although genetics do count for more than you might think. With a puppy, you can ensure from the start that he's getting the right training, the right nutrition, and the right health care.

Remember, though, that puppies need lots and lots of attention. Also, Labrador puppies are notorious chewers, and unless you are willing to carefully supervise your Labrador puppy constantly, you might be better off with an adult who needs a loving home. In addition, an older dog's character is largely established. If you spend some time with him, you'll know more about your prospective new dog than you will by visiting a puppy. And let's not forget housetraining; if you want a dog who is already housetrained, think of adding a needy older dog to your family.

Another decision you must make is whether you'd rather own a male or female Labrador Retriever. This is purely a subjective matter. Some say females are more trainable, while others believe they are less so. Many experts agree that males learn in a more predictable way, but females may actually be able to top them if you are willing to be a bit more flexible in your training methods. In general, male Labs tend to be a bit more slobbery, over the top, and goofy. However, some claim they are more stable and less prone to mood swings. A few males may want to challenge you for dominance in the house as they approach adolescence, something females are less likely to do. Some males also tend to mount everything from their stuffed toys, to your leg, to the family cat. Overall, females tend to be more cultured and understated than males. They give more subtle clues to their needs and hope you're smart enough to figure out what they are.

No matter what Labrador you choose, remember that getting a dog is a solid commitment for the next 10 to 15 years. Neither moving, having a baby, nor sending the kids to Harvard are excuses for getting rid of the dog. And even if you are buying a Labrador partly to be a playmate for your child, remember that you are the one who is responsible for making sure the dog receives adequate food, exercise, and health care.

Breeders

The decision whether to purchase a puppy or adult Labrador is one that should be carefully researched and discussed with the entire family.

Breeder Pros and Cons

If your heart is set on a puppy, your safest bet is to visit a responsible breeder. This may not be the person down the street or

someone who advertises in the newspaper. A responsible breeder is someone whose first and usually only interest is breeding the best Labradors she can. Her goal is to improve the breed, and she wants every litter to be an improvement upon the parents. Responsible breeders are active in the world of Labrador Retrievers and participate in a variety of activities, including hunting, showing, tracking, agility, field trials, or obedience.

One of the great things about breeders is that you often have a chance to observe all of the dogs in the litter with their mother. The sire may not be on the premises, but remember that each parent contributes half of the genes! If the sire is not present, the breeder should have some photos of him, at least, and tell you some reasons why she selected him as the sire for her litter. The puppy may resemble one parent more than another, resemble both equally, or look like neither of them. But he should look like a Labrador!

The only downside to getting your Labrador through a responsible breeder (aside from finding one) is the waiting you'll probably have to do for your puppy. Most responsible breeders have long waiting lists, and so they have no need to advertise in the newspaper or telephone book. What's the best way to find one, then? The best way to find a responsible breeder in your area is to contact the secretary of your local Labrador club, who may be able to direct you to a member who is planning a litter. When talking with the secretary, ask when the next shows are and plan to be there. To find your local Labrador club, go to the American Kennel Club's website at www.akc.org, or look on the Kennel Club's website at www.the-kennel-club.org.uk.

The Interview

One quick test to tell a good breeder from a bad one is to observe whether she asks you a number of questions. Good breeders are very concerned about where their puppies will go, and they will ask you many questions to determine whether you and your family are a good match for their Labradors.

Selecting a Breeder

One excellent way to find a good Labrador breeder near you is to simply contact the secretary of your local breed club. The club will send out a packet of information about Labradors, as well as a list of breeders. (There's usually a small fee.) These are people who are members in good standing with the club.

Every good Labrador breeder knows this breed backward and forward. She should be able to not only point out her dogs' good points, but she should be able to discuss their flaws as well. For example, a good breeder will be frank and honest with you about the health or temperament problems that she has observed in the dogs she breeds. If she doesn't mention them, be sure to ask specifically about hip and elbow dysplasia, progressive retinal atrophy, heart disease, and epilepsy, all of which have made their unwelcome appearance into this breed. However, it's important to remember that no dog is perfect!

Before you go to visit, ask the breeder if she breeds for show or for field work. Some do both, but most specialize in one or the other. Unless you plan on hunting or participating in field trials with your dog, most prospective pet owners are better off with a bench type Labrador who usually has a calmer temperament. If the breeder says she breeds only pets, a warning bell should ring. She may be breeding very nice dogs, but it's important to check her animals carefully for inherited health problems. It's possible that she may be a "backyard breeder" who doesn't really know much about Labradors.

A good breeder will allow you to observe the mother of the puppies you are considering.

You should be allowed to see the mother of the puppies so you can check her condition and temperament. The sire may not be on the premises, but the breeder should be able to provide a good picture of him (preferably winning something). Most good breeders participate in canine activities such as obedience, conformation, field trials, agility, or rescue. She should be able to explain what she wished to accomplish with this particular breeding, such as improving a particular conformation "fault," improving hunting ability, combining certain desirable traits from two lines, or working to produce dual champions.

Your breeder should also be willing to back up her words with a written contract that includes what she will do if your dog develops any heritable diseases. She also should have had *both* parents of the litter tested. Ask to see papers from the OFA (Orthopedic Foundation for Animals) for radiographs for both hip and elbow dysplasia for both parents. Some breeders will offer statements from their personal vet (who probably took the x-rays), but I wouldn't regard this as sufficient. People at the OFA look at thousands of these x-rays every year and know how to read them. In many cases, hips that look fine to a vet might be considered dysplastic by the OFA. Breeders who tell you their dogs don't need health clearances because they've never had a problem are not telling the truth. Of course, health clearances don't guarantee healthy puppies, but they definitely improve the chances.

Don't Spread Germs

If you are visiting several kennels, please don't go to more than one per day. You can unknowingly spread germs from one kennel to another. Small puppies are very susceptible to disease, as their immune systems are not fully developed.

In addition, all Labradors should be checked for PRA (progressive retinal atrophy), a leading cause of blindness. Your breeder should provide proof that she's done so for the parents within the previous year. This test must be performed by a veterinarian with a special diploma in ophthalmology. (These vets usually have the initials ACVO after their name.) The breeder should also provide eye clearances from the Canine Eye Registry Foundations (CERF) performed within the previous 12 months.

A good breeder can provide references from previous buyers, breeder colleagues, and veterinarians, not just other puppy buyers (although these, too, are welcome). She should also be a member of a local Labrador breed club.

After You've Found Your Breeder

You may have to wait for your perfect puppy. Good breeders have long lines of people waiting for their animals. It may be difficult for you to wait, but it will pay off in the long run, because you will be assured that your breeder has taken the time to breed happy, healthy Labradors. A good breeder will not release a puppy until he is 8 or 9 weeks old; at this point, he should already have had his first set of vaccinations for parvo and distemper.

The breeder should provide a sales contract and papers declaring the puppy eligible for entry into the American Kennel Club, United Kennel Club, Kennel Club, or other registries. However, registration does not indicate that you have a quality dog. All it means it that the puppy's parents were also registered. Most puppies are "pet quality," meaning that the breeder does not believe they have a future in the show ring. If the puppy is sold as "pet quality" ask why. The dog may have a minor fault (wrong color eye rims, etc.) that won't detract from his value as a beloved pet.

Pet-quality dogs are sometimes, but by no means always, cheaper than show-quality dogs. Breeders have different policies about this. Don't believe a breeder who assures you that all the puppies in a large litter are show quality—this is stretching the law of averages. If the breeder is reputable, she will probably insist that all pet-quality dogs be spayed or neutered or sold on a "limited registration" that prevents the registration of any puppies your dog might produce in the future. However, your dog is still fully registered by the AKC and can participate in AKC events. Selling on a limited registration is simply a way for the breeder to protect a breeding line. Only the breeder can reverse limited registration.

Labradors come in three colors from which to choose: black, chocolate, and yellow.

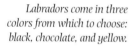

Rescues and Shelters

Rescue and Shelter Pros and Cons

One ethical way to obtain a new family member is to adopt from a responsible Labrador Retriever rescue organization or your local humane society. While most rescued Labs can't offer a dazzling pedigree, these are wonderful dogs who are just waiting for a forever home to show you how much love they have to give. A good rescue makes sure its charges have basic veterinary care and neutering. Their dogs have been in foster homes, so their personalities are known, and many are well trained. Of course, the best advantages of adopting such a dog is that you are performing a kind act that will save more than one life. When you adopt a dog from a shelter, that shelter will have room for one more animal in the future.

AKC Registration

Even though many people believe that a dog registered with the American Kennel Club must be a high-quality dog, this isn't necessarily the case. The AKC is a registry body only, and so your AKC registration certificate does not guarantee the quality or health of the dog. Some AKC dogs are Westminster champions, while others are poor-quality animals of ruinous health and terrible conformation.

While taking in a rescue dog is tremendously satisfying emotionally, it's only truthful to say that it can be hard work, too. After all, you won't be able to show such an animal; he may have phobias, medical problems, or bad habits. Yet this can also be true of even the most well-bred dog. He may also be a much older dog than you planned on having. And although he will certainly be less expensive than a dog from a reputable breeder, you'll end up spending just as much money on him in short order—more if you decide to take in a dog with special medical needs.

Don't be afraid to get an older Lab. Adult Labradors are resilient animals who will bond quickly to your family. They are calm dogs who have usually passed the chewing stage and are longing to spend the rest of their lives in a secure and loving environment. And while some older dogs can have extensive veterinary needs, most are spayed or neutered, have had all their shots, and have passed the age where some really bad hereditary diseases might crop up.

Selecting a Rescue or Shelter

Some rescues and shelters are responsible and some are not, just as with every other source for finding a Labrador. Choosing a rescue that is associated with a national Labrador club is a good option, if you can find one near you. Ask for references or the names of others who have adopted from the rescue.

Be diligent in asking the rescue or shelter relevant questions about the dog's age, health, and temperament. Find out how the dog ended up in the shelter. If he was given up by his former owner, ask if you can contact this person. Chances are that you won't be able to, but it never hurts to ask.

The truth is that no rescue or shelter can give you an iron-clad guarantee about its charges. However, a good shelter or rescue will take the dog back readily if he proves not to be a good fit in your home.

After You've Selected a Rescue or Shelter

A reliable rescue issues a contract the same way a good breeder does. Nearly all rescue groups stipulate that if the dog doesn't suit or can't adapt to your family, you will return him to the rescue, not resell him or give him away. Most rescues also require a home visit and vet check before they will allow you to adopt one of their dogs. The dogs they deal with have already been traumatized; rescue groups want to make sure that the new home will be the last one.

Older shelter or rescue dogs can make terrific pets. Find out as much about their past as possible.

Pet Stores

Some people decide to buy a Labrador Retriever from a pet store. Pet stores can be a convenient option, and they usually offer a wide selection of puppies. It is important to remember, though, that a dog's health, happiness, and well-being are largely dependent on his genetics and the quality of his early care. This is why you must ask the pet store to provide you with all the details of the Labrador Retriever's breeding and history. In fact, pet store employees should be knowledgeable about dogs in general and the breeds they sell in particular.

If you are considering a Lab from a pet store, check the dog for any signs of poor health. A few signs of illness are nasal discharge, watery eyes, and diarrhea. A store should not be selling a dog experiencing any of these symptoms. Even if the puppy seems healthy, be sure to have him checked by your veterinarian as soon as possible. Many health guarantees offered by pet stores are contingent upon a veterinary examination within a few days of the sale.

While you should make every effort to select a Lab based on the criteria that match your lifestyle, sometimes a puppy will just choose you.

CHOOSING THE RIGHT LABRADOR FOR YOU

Physical Appearance

All Labradors look more or less alike—after all, that's what makes a breed! If you have a preference for color, you have black, yellow, and chocolate from which to choose. Some Labradors are rangier than others, but this is a matter of his ancestry and your personal preference. If you're looking at a puppy, you'll want a dog who appears solid (but not fat), with bright eyes, pink gums, and sweet breath. Look for a puppy who moves well and confidently but who is attentive to human beings as well as to his littermates.

If you are adopting or purchasing an adult Labrador, ask permission to take him to your veterinarian for a thorough physical checkup before you sign the contract. A good breeder or rescue will insist that you do. Also, be sure to ask for all veterinary records.

Temperament

While formal temperament testing is best left to the experts, you can do a simple test yourself that gives you a rough idea as to whether or not a particular puppy has a good "pet temperament." Some wonderful show- or field-prospect dogs may be a bit too much "on the muscle" for the average pet owner. (The demands of the show ring, or especially the field, require a dog to be alert and "up" most of the time.) Lower-key dogs often make the best pets.

Watch the puppies move. While you can't tell too much at this stage, a well-moving puppy is a good sign. Pick up the puppy of your choice and cradle him on his back in your arms, just the way you'd hold a baby. It is best to sit on the floor for complete security. He may struggle a bit and that's okay, but a real fighter may be too independent to be the ideal family pet. As you hold him, see if he makes eye contact with you. A dog who won't make eye contact may grow up to be too timid. The adult Labrador should have many of these same characteristics. Overall, he should be friendly and confident, with no trace of viciousness or shyness.

If you are dealing with a breeder, she may have done a temperament test on the litter and will be glad to share the results, but I have some doubts about their efficacy. If performed at the wrong time (even by a day or so, according to some authorities) or by the wrong person in the wrong way, they will yield little information. Your best bet is to observe the puppies yourself. How do they react to each other? To strangers? To their breeder? A good puppy is friendly and not too independent, but he is not shy, either. He should explore his surroundings but also enjoy being held and comforted. If he falls asleep in your arms, that's not a bad thing!

Allow the breeder to help you select the right dog. She's been observing you while you have been observing the puppy. At this point, she should know about you, your family, your lifestyle, and your goals, and she probably has an idea of what pup will work

Choose a puppy with a friendly, even temperament.

best in your home. It helps if you know your own mind as well. Are you looking for a pet, a hunt prospect, or a show dog? Are you interested in obedience, agility, or just wandering around the dog park? Be as honest as possible, and you'll end up with a better dog for your home.

PAPERWORK

One bit of paperwork that comes with a purebred Labrador Retriever is a pedigree, which is really just a family tree of your dog.

In the United States, you will receive the puppy's registration certificate properly filled out by the seller or his application for registration, a copy of the pedigree, and a record of his vaccinations and dewormings. All items should be dated and signed. When you complete your portion and submit it with the proper fee, this form will enable you to register the dog, and you'll receive an AKC Registration Certificate. Paperwork should include the following.

For a Dog Not Yet Individually Registered:
- Breed
- Sex, color, and markings
- Date of birth
- Litter number (when available)
- Names and numbers of sire and dam
- Name of breeder
- Date sold or delivered

For a Registered Dog:
- Breed
- Registered name
- Registration number
- Date sold or delivered

You should also receive some written care instructions, including the kind of food the puppy is accustomed to eating and how much and how often. In most cases, the breeder will give you a supply of the food to tide you over until you can buy some yourself. You may also receive a favorite toy or some of the bedding the puppy is used to.

A breeder will also supply a sales contract that includes the terms under which the puppy is sold.

BRINGING YOUR LABRADOR HOME

Bringing your new Labrador home is a thrilling event! Although you'll usually have your Lab safely crated or protected by a seatbelt during transport, try to get someone else to drive during this first trip home while you cuddle up in the back seat with your precious new companion. Because he is liable to be nervous or even frightened, this is the time to hold him close and speak lovingly to him. In no time at all, he'll probably be asleep!

Do enjoyable things with your puppy the first few days he's in his new home, but keep the playtime relatively calm, and make sure he gets enough sleep.

Settling In

Your dog should have a special place he can call his own, away from noise, traffic, and running children. It can be a crate (with the door open or closed) or a dog bed.

Dog behaviorist Laura Hussey offers a great suggestion for calming your dog at night. She says, "If you have a dog who has a hard time settling down, one who seems to jump up to investigate every noise or movement, try teaching that dog to calm himself by using a technique bird owners use: a cage cover. Bird owners often calm a bird by placing a towel or other covering over the bird's cage. The same principle works pretty well with young dogs when a sheet or beach towel is draped over a crate to muffle outside stimulation. Dogs who learn to calm themselves are much easier to take places and to be around in general."

Establishing Routines

Both puppies and older adopted dogs really rely on regular routines and structure to build their confidence and give them a sense of security. A dog who never knows when he's going to be fed next will be constantly whining for dinner. A dog who never knows when walk time is will demand to go out all the time. A dog who is uncertain when he gets to play with you will be forever begging you to play a game. This doesn't mean that you can't ever forget the routine or give him extra attention; it does mean, though, that he should expect certain things at certain times. Although it may seem like a chore to develop a fixed routine for your puppy, in the long run it will make life a lot easier for both of you.

Enforcing rules consistently from the time your Labrador is a puppy will make it easier for him to learn. Saying no is sometimes harder on the owner than it is on the dog!

Elementary Training

Your new dog, whether puppy or adult, should learn the following things about your house within the first few days:

- Where his food and water dishes are
- When he gets fed
- Where his crate or bed is located
- When he gets to go out
- When people get up and go to bed
- Where his toys are

Knowing these things will help make him comfortable and confident. Dogs whose schedules are switched, food bowls moved around, and who are subjected to varying times for walks have more trouble housetraining and just figuring out their place in the world.

In most cases, your Labrador will figure things out on his own, but if he's having trouble, you may have to show him. Soon, he'll figure out the word "no." He'll hear it often enough. But never let "no!" be the end of your training. If your Lab is doing something you don't want, such as eating your hand or chewing your shoes, offer him a replacement item. Puppies have to do something; they are not stuffed animals. Unfortunately, most of the things they can think of to do are dangerous or damaging. You are the human, and you are the smart one. Thus, you need to figure out something your dog can do that is not damaging or dangerous. This almost inevitably requires you to interact with them!

Most important is that your puppy learns that you are a trusted, loving, gentle leader. If you can get that across, everything else is a piece of cake.

SUPPLIES

While your Lab came into the world with practically nothing, he'll need plenty of possessions to keep him safe, healthy, and occupied. Part of the fun of dog owning is to supply the stuff!

The Rules

You may not think so, but dogs thrive on routine. That's why it's important to establish house rules for your dog that your family will follow. These include feeding times and place; exercise times; placement of beds, bowls, and even leashes; and consistency in training.

A Great Crate

Your Lab's crate, when properly outfitted and used, will become his safe haven—and your place to keep him safe when traveling or entertaining. Crates come in different styles and sizes, and it's important to choose the right one for your Lab. A crate that folds down when not in use is particularly handy.

Food and Water Dishes

Because your Lab will need a constant supply of clean fresh water at all times, as well as regular meals, he'll need his own set of dishes. The best are stainless steel dishes—they are inexpensive, tough, and easy to clean. Ceramic dishes are prettier, though, and they are also suitable, although they can crack. Both come in weighted varieties that resist tipping over by a playful puppy.

I don't recommend plastic dishes for two related reasons. First, Labradors can and will chew through cheap plastic, and second, plastic can develop cracks and gaps that harbor dangerous bacteria.

Whatever style of dish you choose, wash them frequently in hot soapy water, just as you would your own crockery.

The Crate: Your Lab's Lair

Next to eating, sleeping is number one on the agenda of most Labs, and a crate is a safe, comfortable place for that activity. Although crates may look like a cage, a properly trained Lab has no such misconceptions. He thinks of the crate as a safe haven—a den of his own. In addition, a crate is a great housetraining tool.

A crate is not a place of banishment or a baby sitter, though, and dogs should not be kept in their crates for more than two hours except at night when they're sleeping. This doesn't mean your dog has to sleep in a crate, of course. Mine never do. But he should be taught to accept a comfortable crate when asked. This is important for traveling, or when the dog is sick and needs to have his activity restricted, or when you want to keep him away from Cousin Mabel's bratty kids.

Crate Styles

Crates come in three basic styles: wire mesh, sturdy fiberglass or plastic, and fold-up nylon mesh. Each has its distinct advantages, and many dog owners eventually end up with one of each. Size is of critical importance, though. Your Lab's crate should be not only high enough for him to stand up in, but also big enough for him to turn around in easily and stretch out in completely.

- **Wire crates** offer the best ventilation and vision. Once inside, your dog can look around and see what's happening. This type of crate is wonderful in the summer in terms of ventilation. On the other hand, it offers no protection from the sun (unless you drape it with a towel) or cold wind.

- **Fiberglass or plastic crates** like the Nylabone Fold-Away Den & Carrier, are very tough and are perfect for traveling and sleeping. They also provide the most den-like atmosphere, and many dogs feel especially secure in them. The biggest problem with them is that most have reduced ventilation and so aren't desirable when the weather is warm.
- **Fold-up nylon mesh crates** are indispensable for traveling and quick setup. They can go anywhere! Their main disadvantage is that a dog not used to crates can tear them with his claws.

Whatever crate you and your dog choose, be sure to provide a soft, cushy, washable mat for your dog's sleeping comfort. (When you are housetraining, however, you may want to omit the mat—dogs are often driven to urinate on soft, absorbable surfaces for obvious reasons.)

The best food and water dishes are those made of stainless steel, because they are inexpensive, sturdy, and easy to clean.

Bed

With all of the great dog beds out there, most dogs still prefer the couch—or your own bed. Whether you indulge them in their taste is up to you. However, dogs who are territorial or dominant should be required to sleep at ground level. Some dogs equate height with status and power.

Baby Gate

Baby or specially designed dog gates are essential for keeping the dog out of any room you don't want him in. Don't get a wooden gate, though, as your Labrador will chew right through it.

Because you will need to block off certain rooms and the stairway, you should choose a baby gate that's approved by consumer organizations. You can even purchase some made especially for dogs!

Exercise Pen

This portable puppy playpen is a compromise between the isolation of the crate and the free range of the kitchen or living room. During times when you want your puppy near you but not underfoot, the so-called x-pen ("x" is for "exercise") is a great way to oversee his activities. While you are cooking dinner or cleaning the refrigerator, your puppy can watch you. Even more importantly, you can keep an eye on him. Watch for those telltale squirming signs, and you can use the x-pen as a housetraining tool as well as a containment device.

Collar

Your dog should wear a buckle collar and ID tag at all times. Collars are lifesavers—literally. In case of emergency, your Lab can be held and safely restrained by his collar. Most importantly, a collar carries that indispensable ID tag. Although I also encourage you to get your dog microchipped, a lost dog with visible identification is most likely to be returned to his owner.

Adjust your Lab's collar so that you can insert four fingers under it, and if you have a puppy, check it frequently to make sure it's big enough.

Plastic crates are tough and perfect for traveling and sleeping.

Choke Collars

The biggest debate surrounds the use of choke (slip) collars. Unfortunately, the incorrect use of these devices can result in a neck injury, especially for a puppy. Some trainers object to the "punishment" aspect of choke collars, maintaining that owners will achieve better, longer lasting results using positive reinforcement techniques and plain old buckle collars. In my opinion, the less force (or correction) you need to train your dog, the easier the training, and the closer the bond between you and your dog will be. I would begin training with a flat buckle collar.

Head Halters

The head halter is an alternative to a conventional collar. It is humane and safe and works by controlling the head so that the body will follow. People have been leading horses around with halters for centuries; a dog-sized version isn't too different. Proper fitting is really essential, though. One drawback to the halter is that it can only be worn when there is human supervision; left alone, your puppy can get it caught in something as he explores his surroundings. In addition, many dogs may fight it, possibly because they can't put their heads down and sniff around with the ease to which they are accustomed. While most dogs become acclimated to the collar in just ten minutes, others may not adapt as quickly. The fact is that a lot of dogs really dislike the things, no matter how humane they are.

Harnesses

Some people prefer harnesses, especially for puppies. Harnesses are also good for dogs with spinal problems or for sensitive dogs who don't like collars and head halters. They are very safe but provide less control than other methods. However, there are some exceptions. One new harness developed by Wayne Hightower has a loop low on the front at the bottom of the chest instead of along the back, which makes walking a breeze.

Leash

You should also have a regular 4- to 6-foot leash made of leather, waxed cotton, or nylon. Chain leashes are noisy, heavy, and unnecessary. They give no warning when they are about to break, and they can develop sharp edges. Good leather leashes are

Microchipping Your Labrador

You should get your dog microchipped as a second line of defense. The microchip is a pellet the size of a rice grain. It is slipped under the skin between the shoulder blades. The chip can be "read" by humane societies, animal shelters, and many vet clinics. The American Kennel Club keeps a database of microchipped dogs.

durable and comfortable, especially as they age. Beware of cheap leather leashes, however, which can be rough on your hands. The downside of leather leashes is that they are slow to dry out once they get wet. They are also attractive to dogs' taste buds. Never let your Labrador take the leash in his mouth. Once he gets a taste for it, you're doomed. (Some owners spray their leather leashes with a bitter apple spray or a similar aversive product to discourage chewing.)

Teach your puppy to accept the lead by leaving a short one on him for a while. Supervise him the entire time so that he doesn't catch the lead on anything or chew it to pieces. He will probably fuss with it a bit at first, but he'll soon get used it. When you do pick up the end, follow him for a while. When you take the lead yourself, call the puppy to you gently; when he toddles up to you, give him a treat and praise him. Very soon he will be happily following you everywhere. At this stage, try not to struggle with your puppy. If he resists, don't tug the other way, but don't give in either. Lure him to you with a biscuit. He'll soon catch on that it's fun to do what he's asked. Keep puppy lessons short—five minutes a couple of times a day is enough.

Use a 4- to 6-foot leash made of leather, waxed cotton, or nylon.

Pooper-Scooper

Several varieties of pooper-scoopers are available. The advantage of a pooper-scooper is that it saves your back and keeps your nose distant from the object you are picking up. On the other hand, a pooper-scooper is never around at the right time, and it can be a little awkward to carry. You can purchase little baggie pooper scoopers at any discount retailer, but a plain old sandwich bag works just as well and is much cheaper.

Toys

Select toys that are safe, interesting, washable, and durable, such as Nylabones. Of course, what fascinates one dog

Give your Labrador puppy toys that are safe, interesting, and durable.

may leave another cold, but you generally can't go wrong with something that allows a dog to safely chew it and perhaps makes some heartrending noise in the process. Avoid anything with a battery—even a carefully supervised dog can swallow a battery quicker than you think, and then your dog is in serious trouble.

Never give a puppy a toy he can swallow. I don't like rawhides for this reason. Some dogs try to tear large pieces off, partially succeed in swallowing them, and then choke. Many rawhides also contain questionable ingredients, especially if they come from places like Thailand, where there is no governmental regulation. As your puppy grows, he can handle harder toys, but never give him anything harder than tooth enamel. This includes hard dry bones and smoked cow hooves. Both of these items are leading causes of tooth breakage in dogs.

Avoid laser pointers as toys. Although they are intriguing, they can be dangerous. This is because while the pointer offers a continual target, it never gives the dog the opportunity to seize the prey. This sets up a kind of frustration that can evolve into obsessive-compulsive behavior.

It's also a good idea not to offer too many toys at once. You might overwhelm your dog, or you might just succeed in boring him. It's usually best if you rotate your dog's toys. Give him a few to play with, and keep the rest in the closet until you are ready to swap them.

Medical Supplies

The following items, many found right in your medicine cabinet, will be helpful to have on hand. (See Chapter 8 for a complete first-aid kit list.)

- Peroxide
- Antibiotic cream
- Rectal thermometer
- Visine for eye irritation
- Benadryl in case of insect bite or sting
- Petroleum jelly
- First-aid booklet for dogs

Rotate your dog's favorite toys so that he doesn't get bored.

Grooming Equipment

No self-respecting Labrador wants to appear ungroomed, so be sure you have the proper set of grooming tools. A good grooming set should include a wire slicker brush, a short-haired rake, combs (with both narrow- and wide-spaced teeth), and a bristle brush. (Labs do best with a bristle brush, preferably one that has natural bristles.) A rubber curry comb also comes in handy with short-haired dogs like the Lab when shedding season comes around (which is pretty much all the time). And of course you'll need dog nail clippers, shampoo, and dental supplies. For more grooming information, see Chapter 5.

PUPPYPROOFING YOUR HOME: ETERNAL VIGILANCE

Labrador puppies have a lot of energy and a lot of curiosity, and these traits make for a dangerous combination. They have a natural need to explore their world, but they'll require your guidance and supervision. In this way, they are just like toddlers. Close supervision is the only answer, and when you aren't supervising your puppy, he will have to be crated. It's your job to keep your puppy safe!

Indoors

Dogs don't know anything about the dangers of electrical wires, plastic bags, open fireplaces, toxic plants and chemicals, and steep stairs. To puppyproof your house, crawl around on all fours to get a dog's-eye view of the place.

Labradors are famous chewers, but they tend to chew only four kinds of things:

- Expensive things
- One-of-a-kind sentimental, irreplaceable things
- Brand-new things
- Dangerous things

Keep this in mind. Your job is to keep these items out of reach, or if feasible, soak them with a bitter-tasting anti-chew product.

Supervising your child and your dog when interacting together will help everyone remain safe and happy.

Electrical Cords

Both puppies and small children can chew on electrical cords, a dining adventure that is dangerous and even life threatening. Do everything you can to not leave cords exposed. Tack electrical cords close to walls where they won't be conspicuous. If your puppy starts chewing on them (and he will if he can), he can get mouth burns or an electrical shock. Extension cords, which trail across the center of the floor, are especially tempting. You can run cords through spiral cable wrap, cord concealers, or even use PVC pipe to keep them safe from your puppy. You can also spray cords with substances like a bitter apple spray to discourage your puppy.

Furniture

Puppies can get squeezed between sofa cushions, run into furniture hazards that you never thought of until too late, and may get their tails caught under chairs. Your Labrador will want to follow you wherever you go, and it's very easy for you to forget this and close the door on him by mistake. Of course, doors and windows to the outside should remain closed. Stairs should be closed off with a baby gate.

Children and Puppies

One of the most common dangers to puppies is children. Even the best-behaved child can step on a dog or fall on him. Less well-behaved children pull tails, scream, and chase dogs. These behaviors are especially dangerous with puppies, who are not only more fragile than adult dogs, but whose opinion of people, especially little people, is just forming.

It's up to you to socialize both your child and your dog, so be sure to supervise them when they are together, and keep each member of the play team safe and happy. Let your puppy have a safe refuge (like his crate) to go to when he is tired of playing, and make sure your child knows that your dog's crate or bed is off-limits.

Human Food

Not all human food is bad for your dog. Much of it is better than dog food, actually, but there are some notorious exceptions.

Chocolate is found naturally in the cocoa plant and somewhat more unnaturally in your cupboard and refrigerator. It contains theobromine (a compound similar to the caffeine in tea and cola), which can be toxic to canines. Dark chocolate is about nine times more potent than milk chocolate, with baking chocolate the worst of all. Signs of chocolate poisoning include vomiting, diarrhea, frantic activity, rapid pulse, and frequent urination. In a worst-case scenario, coma and death can result.

Other dangerous human food items include onions, alcohol, coffee, tea, grapes, xylitol (an artificial sweetener), and macadamia nuts. Any food that is really high in fat or salt should also be off limits. Walnuts may also be toxic to dogs. Fresh walnuts won't hurt your dog, but moldy old walnuts can contain toxins that cause tremors and seizures.

Leftover food, such as chicken bones, meat trimmings, and the like, are an instant draw for dogs, but these can be dangerous as well. They can cause vomiting, diarrhea, pancreatitis, perforated intestines, and so on. Put these scraps in the trash right away.

Kitty Litter (and Its Contents)

Put the kitty litter box out of reach, perhaps behind a baby gate or in a separate room with a special cat door. Most dogs eat cat feces when they can. Not only can feline feces harbor disease, but the litter that coats it can cause an intestinal obstruction.

Liquid Potpourri

Pleasant as it is to the nose (especially when it dispels some unwelcome dog odors), the essential oils and cationic detergents in liquid potpourri can irritate your dog's gums and intestinal tract if he ingests it. Even exposure to the skin can result in pain, redness, swelling and ulcers. Some dogs will vomit and develop breathing problems, low blood pressure, or weakness. Treatment will depend upon how badly the animal is affected. If the skin was exposed, bathe it with lukewarm water to remove any potpourri that may remain. Pain medication, anti-inflammatories, or antibiotics may also be necessary. Wash the eyes thoroughly as well. Since corneal ulcers can form from exposure to hot liquid, you'll want to take your dog to the vet. If he actually eats the stuff, he may get burns in the mouth or throat. Give him milk or water to drink and take him to the vet. The best cure, though, is prevention.

Trash Cans

Trash cans, including the bathroom wastebasket, should be put behind closed doors or in dog-proof containers. Disposable razors and soap slivers don't belong in your Labrador's stomach. Speaking of the bathroom, keep the toilet bowl lid closed so the puppy doesn't start drinking the water. (For some reason, many Labradors prefer toilet water to their water dish.) If you're not sure

While some human food is good for your dog, other food may be potentially deadly.

53

you can remember to do this, at least refrain from using one of those convenient but dangerous automatic toilet bowl cleaners, which are probably carcinogenic or poisonous.

Drugs

Both prescription and over-the-counter medications can be dangerous to your dog. Please keep all medications (including "harmless" supplements) in a safe, dog-free area. Labradors are not deterred by childproof containers; they will simply crunch up the whole bottle.

Outdoors

Puppies can get into just as much trouble outside as inside, so young dogs need constant supervision while they are in the yard.

Please fence your yard. Even the happiest, most secure Labrador may be seized by wanderlust at any time, so a sturdy fence is essential to your dog's safety. If your dog is a digger, you may actually need to pour a concrete curb along the base of the fence or bury the fence several inches below ground. You can also bury cinder blocks a foot underground right by the fence.

Although some people swear by electronic fences, my own preference is for a conventional fence that not only keeps your dog *in*, but also keeps other dogs and neighborhood bullies *out*. Some dogs, if given sufficient motivation, will even tear through an electronic fence. And once they're out, they tend to stay out, unwilling to risk another shock to get back in. A standard fence doesn't require electricity, special collars, or depend upon electric shocks to confine your dog. Whatever kind of fence you choose, however, make sure that it is high enough to keep your dog from jumping or climbing over it, and low enough to keep him from squirming under it. Be sure to padlock any outside gates to keep out dognappers and thoughtless kids who might think it's funny to let your dog escape. Even the best-fenced yard, however, if not properly monitored and maintained, can be dangerous.

One of the best ways to keep your dog happy at home is to make sure he is happy. Bored, lonely dogs have the greatest need to escape, so spend plenty of active playtime with your pet. When he realizes the best times in his life are the times he spends with you, he'll be less inclined to want to leave. If your dog must spend some part of the day alone in the yard, give him plenty of interactive toys, and don't leave him out there too long. Free run of the yard is no substitute for your company. Your dog needs both.

Rat and Mouse Poison

Unfortunately rat poison tastes as good to dogs as it does to rats; that's why it works. Many of the most common rat poisons contain warfarin, coumafuryl, pindone, valone, diphacinone, chlorophacinone, bromadiolone, or brodifacoum. These are anti-coagulant rodenticides that cause the animal to bleed to death internally if ingested. Remember, these names are the chemical ingredients, not the product names. If you even suspect your dog has eaten this palatable poison, get him to the vet. With vitamin K therapy, which must continue as long as there are toxic levels of the stuff in the liver (usually about three weeks), your dog will probably recover. Another kind of rat poison is bromethalin, which hits the nervous system. There is no cure for this poison, only supportive treatment. Still other rat poisons are strychnine, which induces seizures, and zinc phosphide, which damages red blood vessels. There is no antidote for zinc phosphide.

To obtain the best treatment for your Lab, your vet must know what your dog swallowed. Bring any suspect package with you to the emergency clinic. Signs (especially for toxins in the anti-coagulant class) can be delayed for days, and by the time they appear it may be too late. The best cure is prevention.

Curious puppies need to be protected from exposure to environmental toxins.

Snail and Slug Bait

Snail bait is a common cause of poisoning among dogs. It smells and tastes sweet, making it especially attractive. Although not usually fatal with good vet care, it often requires hospitalization. Symptoms include drooling, tremors, and seizures.

Antifreeze

Almost 10,000 dogs a year die from antifreeze poisoning. Don't let yours be one

Even though Labs are good swimmers, they should still be closely supervised when in the pool.

of them. This sweet-tasting substance is extremely toxic, even in small amounts. Although new, less toxic kinds of antifreeze, based on propylene glycol, are now on the market, many people continue to use those with an active ingredient of ethylene glycol. When metabolized, this chemical depresses the central nervous system and enters the cerebrospinal fluid, making the dog act as if he is drunk. It can also do irreparable damage to the kidneys. Unfortunately, symptoms may not appear until 12 or more hours after ingestion. Untreated it is almost always fatal, but if caught early enough, an antidote can be effective.

Keep your dog away from your garage, and wipe up all antifreeze spills. Of course, if your dog runs loose all over the neighborhood, you have no control over what he might lap up.

Swimming Pools

While Labradors are superb swimmers, they can drown in the family swimming pool if not supervised. Pools should be fenced off from curious dogs who find them absolutely irresistible, especially when the solar cover is on. Solar covers cannot bear a Lab's weight, and if your dog gets trapped underneath, he could drown. Your Lab puppy will almost inevitably jump into the pool and then perhaps panic when he finds he can't get out. In the best-case scenario, he'll claw your expensive vinyl liner to pieces. At worst, he'll drown. Hot tubs should also be covered when not in use.

Pesticides

When used according to directions, most fertilizers and pesticides are harmless to your dog. Trouble arises when your curious Lab comes into close contact with the concentrated product. For example, if your dog walks over dewy grass or garden soil that has been freshly sprayed, he can absorb the chemicals right through his skin or foot pads. If the dog rolls in freshly sprayed grass and then licks himself, he can ingest the stuff. Moss killer is especially hazardous.

If you use a poison to kill insects and your curious dog eats the bugs, he's also ingesting the poison. Please use nontoxic, hormonal, and organic products, but even then it's better to keep your dog away from sprayed areas for at least 12 hours. Nighttime is especially dangerous, because dew reabsorbs the chemicals and makes them available to your dog. Some products are "registered" as safe around pets. If you have concerns, though, contact your vet or the manufacturer. Any label that reads "keep away from children" also means keep away from pets.

Signs of chemical ingestion include:
- Vomiting or loss of appetite
- Impaired balance
- Panting
- Twitching, drooling, or foaming at the mouth
- Seizures
- Diarrhea
- Abdominal pain
- Weakness or paralysis
- Coma

Outdoor Dangers

The friendly garden mulch or compost pile can contain dangerous molds and bacteria, so it's important to keep your dog away from it.

Plant and Garden Dangers

Not all plants are deadly to Labradors, of course, but many are. It's very important to know what you're planting, and while older dogs generally leave plants alone, curious Labrador puppies will chew anything. Labradors have been known to actually devour landscaping stone, which can cause serious intestinal blockage.

Hibiscus and the Easter lily can cause kidney failure in cats and loss of fluids in dogs. Mistletoe causes digestive upset and heart

Although Labradors love the snow, it's important that they not be left outside for too long in extreme temperatures.

arrhythmia. Dieffenbachia (dumb cane) contains oxalate crystals that can cause swelling of the tissues of the mouth and throat. Other poisonous plants include almond, amaryllis, apricot pits, autumn crocus, begonia, bleeding heart, caladium, castor bean, sacred bamboo, chokecherry, daffodils, delphinium, foxglove, hydrangea, jack-in-the-pulpit, jimson weed, kalanchoe, lantana, lily of the valley, marijuana, milkweed, morning glory, oleander, peach pits, philodendron, rhubarb leaves, rosary pea, shamrock, and yew.

Snakes

Because Labradors are nosy and interested in things of the earth, they are at risk in areas where poisonous snakes abide. If a snake does bite your Lab, remain calm. Don't grab a knife, make an X, and start sucking at the (probably) nonexistent venom. Even when a venomous snake bites, it does not always release its venom, which is a precious commodity. In a warning strike, it does not inject venom.

To avoid snakebites, keep your dog on a leash in strange areas, and do not let him dig or explore holes or go beneath woodpiles, a favorite snake hideout. Most snakes are more active at night, especially in warm weather. If you live in an area where there are poisonous snakes, learn to identify them. This helps not only in steering clear of them but also in recognizing harmless snakes that are helpful to the environment. If your dog is bitten, take him to a veterinarian immediately. Call ahead so the vet can get the necessary antivenin from the hospital. Most vets don't keep it on hand.

Seasonal Challenges

Winter

Even though Labradors can handle icy weather, everyone has a limit. Remember that it can be colder outside than the thermometer indicates; wind chill can make it feel many degrees colder than the official temperature. If your Lab spends a lot of time out in the yard, he'll need a shelter. Make sure it's raised off of the ground and contains dry bedding. If the temperatures are extreme, the shelter should be heated or at least well insulated.

Also, don't forget about water. Even though it may not seem as if your Lab is drinking as much in the winter, he'll still need a constant supply of clean, fresh water. You may want to buy a thermal heater to make sure the water source doesn't freeze. Snow is not a suitable substitute, by the way, and licking snow can dehydrate your dog. This is because the snow has to be melted (in this case) in the mouth before it can be used. Snow is also so cold that it lowers the body temperature.

Labradors like nothing better than charging around in the snow, and chances are he'll head for his favorite nearby lake or stream. Be careful, because he can easily jump onto a frozen surface and plunge through the ice. When he tries to come up for air, he'll hit an ice ceiling. To prevent this tragedy, keep your Lab on a leash around ice-covered waters.

If your Lab is outside a lot in winter, especially if he's actually doing important things like hunting or playing Frisbee, he'll need more calories; it just takes more energy to stay alive in the winter. If your dog develops dry, cracked feet, coat them with petroleum jelly. You'll have to keep applying the stuff, as your dog is liable to keep licking it off. However, this is not harmful.

To avoid hazards due to sidewalk salt or extreme cold, consider booties. If your Lab doesn't have booties, dry his feet thoroughly when he comes in from outside. Fungus can develop on wet paws.

Snow Pup

Don't be surprised if your Lab wakes you early on a snowy morning—he wants to get out and play! Labs love running and romping in the snow and will be happy to have you join in their games. Give more food to a Lab who's getting extra exercise in the snow, and remember that snow is not a substitute for fresh water.

Too Hot!

Your Lab will want to go everywhere with you in any season. For his safety, never bring him along in hot or even warm, humid weather if you can't leave the air conditioning on for him in the car. Even with the windows open, a Lab can quickly become fatally overheated in a surprisingly short time. If he does accompany you on a summer picnic, be sure to bring lots of cool, fresh water to keep him cool and hydrated.

Summer

Labradors are cold-weather dogs, and summer heat can pose more dangers to them than winter's icy blasts. Dogs have inefficient cooling systems—they can't sweat. As a result, your Lab needs plenty of shade outdoors in the summer as well as access to clean water. The ideal outdoor temperature for a Lab is 65°F with low humidity. If it gets hotter than this, you will need to monitor your dog's activity level and avoid prolonged exposure to heat and sun to prevent him from getting heatstroke.

Signs of heatstroke include a large, bright red tongue, salivation, and noisy breathing. If you observe these signs, remove your Lab from the hot area and cool him off by pouring cool water over him, and then cover him with wet blankets. Putting some alcohol on his paw pads will help evaporate the water and cool him off. It's crucial that you take your Lab to the vet right away if you see that he is suffering from heatstroke—he may need supportive IV fluids.

The main cause of hyperthermia in dogs is being left in a hot car, even if the windows are cracked. Never leave your Lab unattended in a hot car, even for a few minutes, as the consequences may be tragic.

Cats

While dogs and cats can grow accustomed to each other and even learn to like each other, they are separate species with separate goals in life. While a cat can occasionally scratch or mistreat a nosey dog, by nature of their greater size, dogs can seriously injure or even kill a cat. Thus, it is incumbent on all owners of dogs and cats to make sure that their pets are friends.

The best way to introduce cats and dogs is to do it when they are both young. For dogs, the critical socialization period is between 3 and 12 weeks, while for cats it's between 2 and 7 weeks. This is the ideal, of course, and in real life, many dogs and cats don't get the opportunity to meet each other as youngsters. (Cats mature earlier and have a narrower window of opportunity in this regard than do dogs. In all matters, cats are less flexible and more programmed than dogs, although they are probably just as intelligent.)

If you find yourself in this situation and are determined to keep both pets, you'll need to have distance on your side. A gate that the dog can't jump or push through is essential. Concentrate your efforts on the dog, because the cat will come around if the dog is

calm and friendly. He may never learn to like the dog, but he is unlikely to initiate serious hostile actions. If you have a really savage cat and an utterly peaceful dog, you might consider getting some plastic nail caps that will protect your dog from a scratched cornea. However, please don't declaw your cat. It's unnecessary and cruel.

The best way to introduce dogs and cats is to socialize them to one another while both are still young.

When the dog seems calm and relaxed in the presence of the cat, reward him with a high-value treat, like a bit of cheese. Repeat every time your dog remains calm when the cat is present. Increase the time they spend in each other's presence, and decrease the distance between them. For this to succeed, you'll need to be a strong leader that both pets trust. If you pick up your cat in the presence of the dog and the cat starts to fight and scratch *you*, he doesn't have sufficient faith in your ability to protect him. In any event, your cat should always have a safe place to which he can escape when alarmed or threatened.

If your dog has ever killed or injured a cat, then this prey drive probably cannot be corrected. A strong prey drive trumps training. You may think you have trained your dog out of this drive, but it's only a matter of time and opportunity before he tries again. Don't risk it. While almost all Labradors are perfectly safe around cats, if yours is an exception, he will remain an exception. You will have to

find another home for one of your pets, or you'll need to keep your cat stashed away upstairs in his own quarters.

TRAVELING WITH YOUR LABRADOR RETRIEVER

Traveling with your Lab requires you to be on your best behavior. Keep your Lab on a leash in public, and always clean up after him. If you have to leave the dog alone in your motel room, be sure to crate him. Expect to pay an extra fee, just as you might if you were bringing along an extra person.

If You Go Away Without Him

Alas, you can't always take your dog with you. However, whether you're near or far, your precious Lab trusts you to do the best you can for him in the way of comfort and entertainment while you're gone.

House Sitters

You may be lucky enough to have a trusted friend or family member drop by regularly to take care of your Lab. The ideal person would not only feed, walk, and clean up after him, but also play with him, cuddle him, and perhaps clean the oven. But perhaps that's asking too much. If you can't get somebody to take on the task for free or next to nothing, you might consider engaging the services of a professional house sitter.

Boarding Kennels

Another option is the boarding kennel, but they fill up fast, so you'll have to plan ahead. When you find a potential kennel, call and ask if you can visit. Take your dog along. Not only will you be able to gauge the staff's response to him, but when he returns for his stay, it won't be a completely new experience. Good boarding kennels should feature the following:

- The staff should be polite, friendly, and knowledgeable about dogs.
- The facility should be clean and well ventilated, with large kennels. Beware of overcrowding. Good kennels not only look clean but smell that way, too. Good kennels have heating and air-conditioning.
- The other dogs should be in good condition and look happy.

• The best kennels have convenient hours, are willing to feed your dog his own food (you have to bring it), and will allow you to bring your dog's blanket and toys.

If you decide to take your Lab with you while traveling, be sure to call ahead and make sure he is welcome to stay wherever you plan to go.

Pet Sitters

More than 10 million homes will be visited by a pet sitter this year. For dog owners, pet sitting provides a great alternative to kennels or the maybe not-so-reliable neighbor. A pet sitter will visit your home every day to feed, walk, medicate, and play with your pet. Dogs love the comfort of staying home (even if you're not there), and you will have the comfort of knowing that someone is checking up on the homestead. Pet sitters belonging to Pet Sitters International or a similar organization are bonded, have liability insurance, and are professionally accredited.

Getting a new dog really is thrilling. By doing the things I've described in this chapter, you can make the experience fun and rewarding for you and your Labrador. Your home should be as safe and comforting and welcoming as your heart. If it seems like a lot of work, it is—but it is so worth it!

FEEDING
Your Labrador Retriever

We all need to eat to live, and Labradors live to eat. Labradors are such unpicky eaters, in fact, that dog food companies don't normally use them in palatability tests. Their voracious appetite is a blessing and a curse for the Lab owner. While your dog is likely to plunge into anything resembling a meal with reckless abandon, it's your job to control the amount and make sure that what he eats is of top nutritional quality.

THE BASICS OF NUTRITION

There are six building blocks of good nutrition: water, fats, carbohydrates, proteins, vitamins, and minerals. All animals need these substances! Of these six, five are essential to your Labrador, meaning he will not be able to survive without them. The one building block that may not be essential to dogs (except possibly for pregnant dogs, although this point is debated) is carbohydrates. During the early history of the dog, carbohydrates simply weren't plentiful on the menu, except for perhaps a few berries in the summer. But while carbohydrates aren't usually necessary, they are an excellent source of quick energy.

Water

Keep your dog constantly supplied with clean, cool, accessible water. Some people don't give their dogs enough water when they leave home for the day because they feel that this will make the dog less likely to urinate in the house. If that's the case, please find another way to protect your home. You may want to consider hiring a dog walker or installing a doggy door.

Don't deprive your dog of water. It is cruel and counterproductive. Dogs who don't receive a sufficient amount of water are much more likely to develop bladder and kidney stones. Your dog needs more water than anything else in his diet, and he will die sooner without water than without food. If a dog becomes more than 12 percent dehydrated, he will die.

Fats

Fats have twice the number of calories per gram as do protein or carbohydrates; they are packed with energy. Fats keep cells in good working order, increase the palatability of food, and add texture to food. Dogs digest fats very efficiently, and they need a higher proportion of fat in their diets than humans do to remain healthy.

Dogs can use both plant and animal fats with equal ease. However, oils derived from plants provide large amounts of essential fatty acids (EFAs). These acids are necessary for normal body metabolism to occur. In the wild, dogs eat portions of the vegetable matter contained in the stomach of their prey. This presumably supplies them with some EFAs.

Carbohydrates

Your Labrador should have access to fresh, clean water at all times.

Carbohydrates provide energy and serve as building blocks for other biological components. They are also a heat source for the body when they are metabolized for energy. They can be stored as

glycogen or converted to fat. They also help regulate protein and fat metabolism.

Nearly all commercial dry dog foods are based on carbohydrates in the form of grain and cereal products. As mentioned earlier, dogs can get along perfectly well without carbohydrates in their diet. (There is even some evidence that high-grain diets may be a factor in the development of diabetes, arthritis, and obesity.) What dogs *do* need is glucose, which can be derived from proteins, carbohydrates, or the glycerol found in fats. Your dog needs a steady supply of glucose to keep his central nervous system in good working order. (The body needs glucose so badly that it will get it wherever it can find it, even if it means metabolizing amino acids needed for muscle development.) Thus, a dog on a no-carbohydrate diet needs plenty of protein and fat to make up for it.

Mineral Supplementation

Unless you really know what you're doing, stay away from mineral supplementation in your dog's diet, especially if you have a puppy. Minerals need to be in a particular balance, so if you supplement one, another may become deficient. The most important mineral pairs are calcium/magnesium, calcium/phosphorus, sodium/potassium, and zinc/copper. Speak with your vet or a qualified animal nutritionist before beginning any supplementation program.

Proteins

About 50 percent of every cell in your dog's body is made of protein. Proteins are also critical for building enzymes, hormones, hemoglobin, and antibodies. All animals need protein for maintenance and healing, and young animals need it for growth. If a puppy doesn't get enough protein, his tissues and organs won't develop properly. Like fats and carbohydrates, proteins provide energy. However, all proteins are definitely not equal. Dogs cannot use proteins derived from plants very well; they are carnivores by nature and need high-quality animal-based protein to do their best. Unfortunately, most dog food labels don't tell you where the proteins came from!

Vitamins

Vitamins are plant- and animal-derived substances necessary for your dog's health. A vitamin is defined as an organic component of the diet different from proteins, fats, or carbohydrates. They are critical for normal body functioning, and their absence produces a deficiency syndrome. Vitamins don't have calories, but your dog needs them to convert calories to energy. They also help out with many other jobs throughout the system—everything from helping blood clot to maintaining cell wall integrity.

Vitamins come in two basic types: fat soluble (A, D, E, and K) and water soluble (C and the eight B vitamins). Fat-soluble vitamins need dietary fat in order to be absorbed into the body,

while water-soluble vitamins need only water. The metabolites of fat-soluble vitamins are excreted in the feces, and excess fat-soluble vitamins are stored in the liver.

Water-soluble vitamins (except B12) are not stored in the body and need to be replaced regularly. Most water-soluble vitamins are absorbed in the small intestine and excreted in the urine. Unlike people, dogs don't have a requirement for vitamin C, because they can make their own. However, under times of duress, extra vitamin C has been shown to be beneficial.

Minerals

A dietary mineral is any inorganic component of a food. Like vitamins, minerals are substances necessary to maintain an animal's health. Dietary minerals are generally classed into three groups: macrominerals (sulfur, calcium, phosphorus, magnesium, and the electrolytes sodium, potassium, and chloride), which are consumed in gram quantities per day; trace minerals (iron, zinc, copper, iodine, and selenium), which are needed in milligrams or micrograms per day; and ultratrace minerals (beryllium, etc.), which have been shown to be necessary in laboratory animals but have not been proven to be necessary in dogs.

Minerals participate in nearly every function of the body. They build teeth and bone, serve as parts of enzymes, and are a vital part of the blood and other body fluids. Minerals also play a role in muscle contraction, cell membrane permeability, and the transmission of nerve impulses.

As is the case with protein, dogs can make better use of minerals derived from meat than from plant-derived minerals. This is especially true with zinc, iron, and copper. Plants often contain "anti-nutritional" factors like phytate, oxalate, and certain fibers like beet pulp that can limit mineral availability.

DOG FOOD LABELS

The label on a package of dog food is a legal document. That means it is subject to certain rules. The principal display panel, located on the front of the package, must contain the brand name of the food and the name of the product. It must also state that the food is intended for dogs, in case you were looking for a snack for yourself. In addition, the package will state what life stage the food is intended for—puppy, adult, or senior—or whether it is intended for all life stages.

The labeling then becomes a little more complicated. If the label states that it is, for instance, "Lamb Dog Food" (*food* is the operant word), it must be 95 percent lamb, exclusive of the water sufficient for processing. No dry food meets this standard, but if it uses a word like "dinner" or "entree" rather than "food," it needs to be only 25 percent lamb. If it uses the words "with lamb," it need only contain 3 percent lamb. If the word "flavor" is used, it means that merely the flavor of the food must be detectable to dogs. Nowhere

Where's the Beef?

Unfortunately, almost any kind of meat can end up in dog food. In many places, pet food manufacturers are free to use road kill, cows that have died from disease, or any other source of protein that suits them. Other companies, on the other hand, use only human-grade meat. Formerly, companies were not permitted to state this valuable fact on their labels. However, this regulation has now thankfully been relaxed, so you can easily choose human-grade meats for your dog.

on the label will you find the actual percentages.

Dog food also contains an information panel on the package that includes the guaranteed analysis. The guaranteed analysis is the *minimum* amount of crude protein and crude fat required by the Association of American Feed Control Officials (AAFCO). It also gives the *maximum* levels for crude fiber, moisture, and ash. The minimum percent of protein for maintenance is 18 percent, while the minimum for growth and reproduction is 22 percent. Again, this doesn't specify the actual quality of the protein—just how much is present. The information panel also includes feeding instructions and the nutritional adequacy claim. Last is the list of ingredients.

The AAFCO Seal of Approval

Most dog foods sold commercially in the United States bear the seal of approval of the Association of American Feed Control Officials (AAFCO) indicating that the food in question has passed either an AAFCO feeding trial or an AAFCO nutrient profile. The feeding trial is somewhat of a higher standard, but neither one tells the consumer much about the actual quality of the food. For example, the following describes how a feeding trial is conducted:

- Eight dogs older than one year of age must begin the test.
- At the start of the test, all dogs must be of normal weight and in good health.
- A simple four-panel blood test (not a complete chemistry) is to be taken from each dog at the start and finish of the test.
- For six months, the dogs used must only eat the food being tested.
- The dogs finishing the test must not lose more than 15 percent of their body weight.
- During the test, none of the dogs are to die or be removed due to nutritional causes.
- Six of the eight dogs starting must finish the test.

Unfortunately, this test doesn't take into

consideration the differences among breeds or many other important factors, such as the size of the dog, environmental conditions, degree of exercise the dog receives, etc. It's not multi-generational, either. Thus, while an AAFCO-approved food won't kill your dog, there's also no guarantee that he'll thrive on it. Although most foods sold across state lines bear the AAFCO seal of approval, that doesn't mean it's a perfect food. It means it has met minimum requirements, either through feeding trials or by adhering to "nutrient profiles" obtained from feeding trials.

You'll know that you're feeding a high-quality food if your Lab is the picture of good health and has the right energy level.

Tips on Choosing the Best Food

You can choose the best foods and avoid the worst foods by adhering to some simple guidelines.

- Avoid dog foods containing "by-products." Meat by-products are the part of the animal not deemed fit for human consumption. While some by-products are both healthy and tasty to dogs, many more are not. Avoid them.
- Avoid food laden with grain or cereal by-products. These ingredients are the part of the plant left over after the milling process; they are technically called "fragments," but they appear in many guises on the label. The carbohydrates in food should be whole grains. Many dogs are allergic to soy, so stay away from it.
- Good food should not contain sweeteners, artificial flavors, colors, or preservatives. The best dog foods are preserved naturally with vitamin E (tocopherols) or vitamin C (ascorbic acid). Don't select a food preserved with citric acid. Studies have shown a connection between citric acid and the development of bloat.

Dog food companies used to use ethoxyquin for preserving food. Ethoxyquin was originally developed as a rubber hardener, and later it was used as an insecticide. Although it cannot legally be used to preserve human food (with the minor exception of chili powder), as there is some fairly convincing evidence it causes

There are so many choices in the pet food aisles that it is increasingly difficult to choose the one that's best for your Lab. Think quality over cost or quantity—it pays off in the long run. Foods are made for life stages, too, so look for puppy, maintenance, or senior diets based on your Lab's life stage.

cancer, liver disease, and immune disorders, manufacturers have used it for years to preserve dog food. Because of increasing consumer pressure, the FDA announced in 1998 that ethoxyquin is not safe in dog food, either. It has asked manufacturers to voluntarily stop using it.

- Select food with the specific name of a meat (beef, chicken, turkey) as the first ingredient. Avoid foods with labels that list a generic "meat" or "poultry" rather than the specific meat, like "chicken" or "beef." Unfortunately, just because a product has beef as the first ingredient doesn't mean that the product is mostly beef. Some companies engage in a nefarious practice called "splitting." If they can possibly do so, they will divide the cereal products up into separate categories, like "rice" and then "brown rice." Added together, there may be more rice than beef. But because the companies are allowed to list them as separate ingredients, beef is listed first.

Unfortunately, although dog food labels declare the amount of protein in a food, they don't say where the protein comes from. Plant proteins are much lower in quality than animal-derived proteins, and reading the labels on pet products will leave you guessing about the protein source. To find more detailed information, you'll need to check with the food companies directly.

TYPES OF FOOD

Your choice of what to feed your dog is practically unlimited: dry food, canned food, semi-moist food, "people food," or any mixture thereof. I am not going to tell you that only one kind is right for you and your dog. Many factors come into play: convenience, expense, nutritional value, taste, availability, allergies, and other things. What's right for one dog is not right for all. One rule I do apply is don't feed your Labrador something he dislikes. Yes, he will eat almost anything if he gets hungry enough, rather than starve. So would I, but that doesn't mean I'd like it. Mealtimes should be pleasurable for everyone, so why not shop around until you find something nutritious that your dog really enjoys? If he seems to like something for a while, then gets bored with it, change his food. It's not difficult.

Whatever you choose, go for quality. The difference between the best and worst is just a few dollars a bag, but the difference in nutrition can add healthy years to your dog's life.

Commercial Dog Foods

Humans have been feeding their dogs processed foods, at least on a large scale, since World War II. The military played a role in the popularization of processed foods, because the army needed a convenient, easy-to-store food for its dogs of war. Nowadays, about 95 percent of American dog owners feed their dogs primarily or solely a commercial diet, usually dry kibble. While most commercial dog foods contain the minimum amounts of nutrients to be considered "nutritionally complete," none of them are really ideal foods for your dog. Their greatest advantage is that they are convenient. Some premium products on the market do approximate top nutrition, but these products can be hard to find. You won't find them in grocery stores or even in most pet supply stores. This doesn't mean you can't get them, though. Search the Internet to find a distributor near you, or have the dog food delivered right to your door.

If you have questions about the food you are feeding your Labrador, call the telephone number usually listed on the label. Ask where the meat comes from in the product. In addition, question whether the food is organically grown, and ask if the company

Puppies tend to glow with good health. Tending to their nutritional needs will help keep that glow going as they age and mature.

performs its own feeding trials. (Many smaller companies can't afford them, but larger reputable companies usually do their own.)

Dry Food (Kibble)

Most kibble is largely corn, rice, or soybean based. Better brands contain meat or fish as the first ingredient, and while they cost more, they are actually a better bargain because your dog doesn't need to eat as much of it. Kibble is also more calorie-dense than canned dog food, as canned food contains a lot more water by volume. Large dogs like Labs can actually have trouble getting their caloric needs met on a solely commercial canned food diet, which makes kibble a practical choice for many people.

Canned Food

Although some canned dog food smells unpleasant to humans (one reason most people prefer to serve kibble), most dogs prefer both the aroma and flavor of canned foods. In fact, some people serve such unappetizing dry fare that they have to anoint it with canned food before their dogs will touch it.

Because large-breed dogs can have trouble meeting their caloric needs on a canned food diet alone, kibble is a practical choice.

To find the best canned food for your Lab, check the label. Look for food containing whole meat, fish, or poultry as the first ingredient. Most lower quality canned foods have water as the first ingredient, and many canned foods are more than 78 percent water. The best canned foods use whole vegetables, not grain fractions like rice bran, rice flour, or brewers rice.

Unfortunately, the top canned foods can't often be found at the supermarket; you must go to the manufacturer, a few pet specialty stores, or dog shows. This is because the high shelf rental space of most supermarkets is out of the reach of many small, premium pet food manufacturers.

Semi-Moist Food

There is a variety of food labeled "semi-moist" that comes in little packages. Most of this food looks good, but nearly all of it is bad for your dog. Semi-moist food is *loaded* with sugar in the form of corn syrup and beet pulp (up to 25 percent). It is also made up of about 50 percent water. Your dog does not need this stuff, which promotes obesity and tooth decay. The shelf life of these products is also lower than either canned or dry food.

People Food

Most of what people eat is good for dogs. If you eat a healthy diet of meat and fresh vegetables, cook a little extra for your Lab. If you eat mostly potato chips, chocolate, and chewing gum, your Lab is better off with dog food. Don't let the dog food companies tell you your dog will keel over from malnutrition if he's deprived of a commercial diet. A commercial diet is adequate and convenient, but it certainly does not contain optimal nutrition.

Homecooked Meals and Raw Diets

If you decide to prepare your dog's food yourself, take the time to learn the basics of canine nutrition. This is not something you can do without adequate information, but many excellent books are on the market. For example, a dog fed meat alone will receive insufficient calcium. If not enough calcium is present in the blood, the dog's body will be forced to extract it from the bones, causing a condition called nutritional osteodystrophy. If too much calcium is provided relative to phosphorus, a dog could develop lameness and bone and joint problems.

Many people feed their dogs raw food, and some claim it helps with allergies. This has not been my own experience. If you make your dog's food, cook it the same way you cook yours and for the same reasons: It's safer, it's more digestible, and it's more palatable. Studies have shown that even dogs prefer cooked food (medium rare) to raw. While most dogs can devour raw food and not become sick, there's absolutely no point in taking the chance.

If you decide to feed your dog raw meat, get the freshest cuts available. Because of the new interest in feeding raw diets, the FDA, which does not believe that raw diets are healthier than others, has issued the following guidelines for pet owners who want to try it with their dogs:

Kibble and Brush

It is commonly believed that dry food helps keep a dog's teeth in good condition. There is some evidence that a diet of hard kibble does indeed slow down periodontal problems, but it doesn't stop them altogether. Only regular brushing will keep teeth in good condition.

Variety in Your Lab's Diet

The best single thing you can do to ensure that your dog is getting what he needs is to feed him a variety of different foods. This will not only make eating more pleasurable for him, but it will also help protect him from developing allergies if you start early enough. I also strongly urge you to supply your dog with something besides a steady diet of commercial foods. Well-chosen table scraps will not only reduce your Lab's risk of bloat, but they can boost the quality of every meal.

- Choose meat that has been approved for human consumption by the U.S. Department of Agriculture/Food Safety Inspection Service.
- Choose meat that comes from manufacturers who use measures, such as irradiation, to prevent bacterial contamination of the meat.
- Choose meat from manufacturers who have implemented a hazard analysis and Critical Control Point program designed to pinpoint contamination sources and take action to prevent problems at these sources.
- Choose meats that have been frozen or freeze dried during shipping.
- Choose foods that include ground, not whole, bones.

Manufacturers should include guidelines for safe use with their products that instruct consumers to keep the products frozen until ready to use; thaw the product in a refrigerator or microwave; keep the product separate from other foods; refrigerate or discard unused product; and to thoroughly wash working surfaces, utensils, hands, and any other items that touch the product.

A great deal has been written lately about the advantages of a raw diet. However, it is best to check with your vet before making any major decisions that may affect your dog's diet. There are some disadvantages to feeding your dog a raw diet, even if the meat supply is completely safe. Raw meat harbors organisms that can kill a dog. Common bacterial components of raw meat include campylobacterosis, E. coli, listeriosis, salmonellosis, trichinosis, and tapeworm. Protozoal infections are also possible. Cooking destroys those organisms. While it is true that cooking also destroys some important enzymes as well, dogs actually can make these enzymes themselves, just as humans can.

Don't let anyone talk you into a "natural diet" for your Labrador without first consulting your veterinarian.

Treats

The simplest advice on treats that I can give is to go easy! Labs easily gain weight, and treats add up. The healthiest treats are bits of carrot or apple. You don't have to buy expensive biscuits filled with preservatives and dyes. For a special occasion, a pea-size bit of cheese works perfectly. And, fortunately, the people-loving Lab responds well to hearty praise, too. That's the best treat of all.

Bones

Bones are naturally balanced sources of calcium and phosphorous, and dogs adore them. However, cooked bones are dangerous, because they can easily splinter and damage your dog's throat and digestive system. The sterilized bones you can buy in the store are very dangerous in this regard: They are unnaturally hard and can cause broken teeth. Whole, *fresh* bones are safer, but the best choice is to have the bones thoroughly ground and cooked. Raw bones may carry bacterial dangers of their own, but the nutritional advantages are without par. It is important that the bones be both fresh and meaty for your dog to benefit. Start your

If your Lab receives sufficient exercise, he will be less likely to become obese.

Liver Treats

If you enjoy cooking, you might consider making some healthy liver treats for your dog. Boil a beef liver with just a bit of garlic powder until it is thoroughly cooked. Place the liver on a baking sheet and cook in the oven at 200°F until it is dried out. Then, cut the liver into small pieces and store them in the freezer. These make excellent training rewards.

dog off gradually, and watch him closely. Dogs need to learn to eat bones properly.

Your best choices are raw chicken legs and wings, because these bones have a perfect calcium/phosphorus ratio. Beef and even turkey bones may be too hard.

The most dangerous consequence of bone consumption is a perforated intestine, which allows toxins to escape into the dog's system. When dogs chew bones, they splinter, and splintering bones can puncture the esophagus or stomach. If you want to avoid these risks, give your Lab some safe chew toys instead.

Foods to Avoid

Grapes and Raisins

Reports have recently implicated large amounts of grapes and raisins (between 9 ounces and 2 pounds) in acute kidney failure in dogs, although no one knows exactly why. The kidney shutdown is so dramatic that aggressive treatment may be necessary to save your dog's life. Treatment for animals who have been poisoned by grapes and raisins includes:

- Administering activated charcoal. This helps prevent absorption of the toxic substance, whatever it is.
- Blood tests to evaluate kidney function.
- Hospitalization with intravenous fluids.

Chocolate

Chocolate, especially baker's chocolate, can cause a range of problems, including cardiovascular difficulties and even seizures.

Onions

A quarter cup of onions can induce hemolytic anemia, a severe but usually temporary condition. Serious cases can even require a blood transfusion. Garlic has the same properties, but garlic in very small amounts probably does your dog some good. However, don't rely on garlic as a flea fighter.

Corncobs

Some people think it's interesting to watch their dogs deal with corncobs. It's not. Dogs are not horses, and the cobs can impact the intestines.

FEEDING SCHEDULES

A Lab puppy who is six to eight weeks old should be fed three to four times a day and twice a day thereafter for the rest of his life. He should remain on a large-breed puppy food until he is about a year old.

Feeding the Puppy

Young Labrador puppies (two to four months) need to eat four times a day, usually a high-quality kibble softened with some warm water. You can add yogurt, canola, corn oil, flaxseed oil, or cottage cheese for palatability. From four to six months, you may reduce the number of meals to three per day and reduce this to two meals a day at six months of age. At one year, some people start feeding once a day, although twice-daily feedings seem to please the dog more. Regardless of his age, your Labrador should always have access to plenty of clean, fresh water.

Labs gain weight easily, so healthy treats like bits of carrot or apple are the best way to go.

Feeding the Adult Dog

Labradors reach adulthood between the ages of one year and eighteen months, and at this point they should be fed twice a day for the rest of their lives. If you are feeding a commercial food, choose one of high quality. If you are feeding kibble, you can top it off with a spoonful of yogurt or low-fat table scraps for added taste. Studies show this also helps prevent bloat.

Feeding the Senior Dog

As your Labrador ages, he will become less active, and consequently, he will need fewer calories. Although every individual is different, most Labradors acquire "seniority" at about eight years of age. If you are

Young Labrador puppies should be fed four times a day.

feeding a high-quality dog food, you can safely reduce the amount he eats. Less premium dog foods, however, contain just enough vitamins and minerals to keep your dog going at the amount indicated, so you will have to supplement with vitamins and minerals. Fish oil or glucosamine/chondroitin can be beneficial to many older animals.

However, if your senior dog seems to be doing just fine on his regular diet and he doesn't seem to be losing weight or condition, there's no reason at all to switch him just for the sake of switching. So-called senior dog foods are not required to meet any pre-determined standard, so two different "senior" dog foods may not be equivalent in the nutrition they provide.

Overall, keep in mind that older dogs have special dietary needs. One of the main ones is that they need more protein (unless they have kidney trouble) than young adults. They also benefit from arginine, an essential amino acid for the immune system; omega-3 fatty acids to keep their brains and nervous system in good repair; and less phosphorus to maintain health.

OBESITY AND MANAGING YOUR LAB'S DIET

Hunger is the natural state of all mammals, including dogs. Dogs are naturally programmed to run all day long in honor of the time long ago when they chased game across the tundra. Running takes a lot of energy, so dogs are programmed to eat as much as possible. They never know how long it will be before they catch the next caribou. In fact, today's dogs have the same instinct to gorge as did their ancestors, but almost none of them receive the exercise necessary to work off those extra calories.

Unfortunately, Labs gain weight extremely easily, with neutered females over the age of four most at risk. Obesity is one of the most common nutritional medical disorders of dogs, with 25 to 40 percent of pets classified as overweight. Labradors are on the higher end of that statistic. The reason for this is that these cold-weather water dogs were bred to conserve energy in the bitter winter and water environment. Thus, their metabolism is comparatively slow, and they gain weight easily. This trait was an advantage in the Newfoundland of old but has become a disadvantage in present-day suburbia. Overweight dogs are more at risk for respiratory problems, heart disease, and arthritis—just like people.

Causes of Obesity

The increasing number of obese dogs relates to two important factors: Dogs are more sedentary nowadays, and they eat better foods. Obese dogs are overweight because they take in more calories than they expend, just as many humans do.

And as with people, this is largely an individual thing. Two dogs who exercise equally and are of the same breed, age, and sex may eat the same amount of food, but one will gain weight and the other won't. That's why it's imperative for you to keep tabs not just on how much you feed your dog but on what the dog looks like.

Preventing Obesity

Early dog/owner education is the best way to prevent obesity in dogs. You can also check your dog's weight at home. If your dog is at his ideal weight, you should be able to feel (with a bit of difficulty) the ribs but not see them. You should also be able to see a slight tuck-up at the waist when you view the dog from the side. Perform this test about once a month for adult dogs and once every couple of weeks for puppies.

One way to control your dog's weight is to provide him with the right amount of food for his ideal weight. Your vet can help you to determine how to do that. Of course, the dog food package also contains instructions about how much to feed, but beware. In less expensive brands, owners are often instructed to feed more in order to assure the dog receives sufficient vitamins and minerals.

Use a measuring scoop or cup to be sure you're feeding a consistent amount. You can achieve moderate weight loss in your pet by feeding 10 to 20 percent fewer calories through less volume of regular food. Restricting calories usually reduces vitamins and minerals, however, so make sure your dog is getting a high-quality commercial food that supplies the extra nutrients. You can also feed a vitamin or

Roly-Poly Is Not Cute

Overfeeding puppies is especially dangerous, because it can lead to an overproduction of fat cells. Once those fat cells are there, they stay there. The dog will then always have a tendency to gain weight. In addition, overfeeding may speed up the growth rate, which can lead to abnormal growth of the joint cartilage and other skeletal diseases. An overweight, roly-poly puppy is therefore not desirable.

mineral supplement after first consulting your veterinarian. If you need to reduce your dog's food intake by more than 20 percent for faster weight loss, you should consult your vet. You may need to get a specially fortified food. As with humans, however, it hasn't been determined what kind of weight-loss formula works best. Some weight-loss foods are low in fat with more complex carbohydrates, while others have higher levels of indigestible fiber. Discuss these options with your vet.

Although feeding treats is great fun and a useful training aid, they pack on the pounds. If you do enjoy feeding your dog treats, cut down proportionately on his meals, or give low-calorie treats like carrot pieces.

In some cases, you may want to resort to a commercial low-calorie food. Pick one that includes specific weight-loss directions. (If you feed a dog according to the regular feeding directions, he won't lose weight. Regular feeding directions are designed to maintain a dog's weight.) Canine diet foods are not meant to be fed as a maintenance diet, and they usually contain high amounts of fiber. While fiber helps make a dog feel full, it also reduces the absorption of some nutrients.

A better way to keep your dog's weight in check is to provide him with plenty of healthy exercise. Dogs like this option much better than cutting down on their food, too. If you are starting an exercise weight-loss program for your dog, check with your vet before embarking on anything truly strenuous.

Helping your Lab shed the extra pounds will help him remain healthier and live longer. Research shows that controlling your dog's weight may "reduce" his age as much as 20 percent!

Foods for Big Dogs

Because Labradors are larger dogs, you should feed your puppy a commercial food designed for large breeds. This will help ensure he is getting the proper amount and ratio of calcium and phosphorus. These critical minerals are the most plentiful minerals in the body and are essential for bone development in growing puppies. Big dogs like Labradors can easily develop bone disease when the calcium/phosphorus ratio is disrupted.

GROOMING

Your Labrador Retriever

Proper grooming makes your dog look and feel good. Even the act of grooming helps form a bond between you and your dog. It also serves as a mini-health check, because during the grooming you're more apt to notice lumps, discharges, strange smells, sores, and other anomalies.

GROOMING SUPPLIES

To groom your Lab properly, you will need the following supplies:
- Slicker brush (to remove dead hair and for touchups)
- Steel comb (to remove tangles)
- Curry comb (to remove dead hair and the dirt that is deeply embedded in the undercoat)
- Blunt-edged scissors (for trimming)
- Pet towels
- Shampoo
- Get a tack box to hold all of your supplies.

COAT CARE

Great coat care starts from the inside. For example, if your dog is eating low-fat foods, his coat will tell the tale—it will be dry and rough. A healthy hair coat needs fat to shine at its best. Although frequent and thorough brushing will help bring out your Lab's shiny coat, the real secret is good nutrition. And there is a secret ingredient—the omega fatty acids.

The omegas come in two basic varieties: the omega-6 fatty acids and the omega-3s. The former abound in nature and in your dog's food, as they are found in plant oils like sunflower oil. Even dog foods that don't contain sunflower or safflower oil carry their "precursor," linoleic acid, found in all nationally distributed dog foods. The omega-3s are harder to come by naturally, and so they must be added. Because they are expensive, some cheaper dog foods may not have them. Omega-3s are found in marine fish oil and flaxseed oil, but marine fish oil is more bioavailable to dogs (meaning the dog's body can use it more easily and efficiently).

Most nutritionists believe that the omega-3 and omega-6 acids need to be balanced. The current theory is that the ideal ratio of omega-6 to omega-3 is 5:1. Too much omega-6 in relation to omega-3 may produce an inflammatory response that can dull the coat and even produce an allergic-like itch. Too little omega-6 in relation to omega-3 may weaken the immune system. Quality commercial foods add the omegas in the correct balance.

Brushing

All dogs benefit from a good brushing, and this should be a part of your Labrador's regular grooming routine. Brushing helps improve circulation, stimulate the skin, remove dead hair, and make him feel healthy and loved.

Brushing your Lab will help improve circulation, stimulate the skin, and remove dead hair.

Brush your Lab once or twice a week with a hound mitt or a

soft, natural bristle brush. The bristle brush will help distribute oils evenly throughout the coat, but it isn't very good for getting right down to the skin. A pin brush will do the trick for that! Brush in the direction of the hair growth, and work from the skin out. Use a rubber brush to loosen the dead hair; follow with a bristle brush to take it off. (Some people prefer to use a rake for this purpose.)

Have a regular routine for brushing; this way, you won't forget anything, and your dog will know what to expect. Brush in the direction of hair growth and aim for a flat (not wavy) finish. Begin at the head and work your way down to the tail, using short, gentle strokes. Brush the legs and then move to the tail and under the ears. Finish with the back and sides. These areas are likely to

Controlling the Shed

Shedding is a natural part of doggy life, and Labradors are pretty heavy shedders! You can't stop shedding, but you can control it by taking loose hair off your dog before he leaves it all over the house. Shorter-haired breeds like Labradors actually tend to shed *more* than longer-haired breeds. (That's because shorter hair has a shorter shed cycle. Take human hair—it grows really long, and we don't shed much.)

The trick to keeping shedding under control is regular and thorough brushing. Brushing not only removes dead hair, but it also helps keep the skin and coat in excellent condition. Warm baths and more frequent grooming may help speed up the process. So does a stripping knife, which you can use like a comb; it gets rid of an enormous amount of dead hair.

Dogs shed worst in the spring and fall, although many don't adhere to this natural cycle and shed whenever and wherever they feel like it. Yellow Labs in particular seem prone to shedding year round, while black Labs prefer the twice yearly "coat blow" modality. It's difficult to say which is worse!

During the shedding season, you really need to attack the coat (not the dog—just the coat). The sooner you get the old dead coat brushed out, the sooner and nicer the new coat will come in. Remember that any hair you don't brush or comb out while grooming will end up on your carpet.

Shedding seems to be triggered by hormonal changes that are tied to day length and light conditions. It always seems worse in dry winter months. Unnatural shedding may also be caused by poor nutrition, bad health, or stress (which includes things like surgery and whelping.) In these cases, purchase a product that contains the right combination of omega-3 and -6 oils to help your dog's coat achieve its very best look.

cause the least trouble, so you will finish the brushing on a very pleasant note.

Trimming

If your Lab has hair growing between his pads and around the edges of his feet, take a pair of blunt-edged scissors and trim away the excess. You may want to trim some hair from under the tail near the base to help keep that area more hygienic. Hold the tail out straight and scissor out about an inch to an inch and a half. A grooming table with a noose makes this a lot easier. Otherwise, you may need a friend to help hold the dog.

Bathing

Probably the biggest myth surrounding dog care is that frequent bathing destroys the coat. This is simply not true, any more than frequent shampooing destroys your hair. It is true that frequent use of harsh shampoos can strip away important oils, but the answer to that is not to use harsh shampoos. I have bathed every one of my dogs once a week for many years, and none of them has ever had a problem with dry skin, dandruff, or hotspots. In large part, how

Oatmeal Baths

An oatmeal bath is the perfect solution for pets with dry, itchy skin. You can use a colloidal commercial product that dissolves instantly in water, or you can even use ordinary breakfast oatmeal wrapped in cheesecloth or a sock. You can use oatmeal soap or shampoo as well, although some of these products contain added substances that may irritate the skin further. In general, the fewer chemicals a shampoo contains, the safer it is.

Encourage your dog to soak in a cool tub for at least ten minutes. (Warm water tends to make itching worse.) Bathe your dog every day for three or four days until the itchiness goes away. For smaller itchy areas, use a cool oatmeal compress on the irritated skin. Oatmeal baths and compresses are also excellent for dogs who have been bitten by ants or stung by bees.

much you bathe your Labrador depends on your personal preference. Follow your instinct!

Frequent use of a gentle shampoo will keep your Lab's coat clean and shiny. You can choose either a mild human shampoo or one specially formulated for dogs. The pH of dog and human skin is different, but that doesn't really make a difference as far as shampooing goes. The biggest advantage to using dog shampoo, though, is that it doesn't seem to lather as much and so rinses out more easily. This is important, because if you don't get all of the shampoo out of your Lab's coat, it will dry out and irritate his skin.

Put a drop of mineral oil in each eye to help protect against errant shampoo, and place a cotton ball in each ear to keep the water out. (Water in the ears can lead to infection.) Don't forget to take the cotton balls out when you're done.

To wash the dog, first get him in the tub. Put a non-skid mat on the bottom to ensure that he won't slip. If your dog is hard to control, you can buy an attachment that basically anchors his collar to the wall. Because Labs love the water, though, they aren't as adverse to baths as other breeds.

A handheld shower attachment makes bathing much easier—I wouldn't even attempt it without one. Use three or four units of water for each unit of shampoo; it will lather and rinse better. To really get the shampoo spread around the dog, use a sponge.

Use warm water, not hot, when bathing your Labrador. Start at the head, making a collar of soap around the neck, and work backward. If you shampoo the head, use a tearless shampoo; there are kinds available for dogs. To do the face, apply the shampoo to your hands and work it gently. Lather the whole dog briskly and follow with a conditioner if desired. Then rinse, rinse, rinse, and rinse some more. It should take twice as long to rinse a dog thoroughly as it did to wash him.

Your dog's fur should literally "squeak" if it's clean. If your Lab has oily skin, use a rinse of half water and half witch hazel or apple cider vinegar. Add just a bit of lavender and chamomile. Try this instead of a commercial conditioner; it does a great job of cutting the oil, leaving the dog with a wonderful coat.

Dry your Lab off with thick, absorbent towels. When he jumps out of the bath, he'll start to shake. Because dogs shake from the front, hold his head; that way, he won't be able to shake water all over you.

NAIL CARE

Few dogs enjoy having their nails trimmed, but most learn to tolerate it. It's ideal to start trimming (or even pretending to trim) your dog's feet from the time he is a youngster. Constantly playing with your dog's feet will get him accustomed to the idea— you can't start this too early!

It is best to begin trimming your Labrador's nails at any early age to get him accustomed to the procedure.

While tar isn't likely to kill your dog, it can be a nuisance when it gets caught in fur or paw pads. If your Lab does get tar stuck on him somewhere, use mineral oil or petroleum jelly to soften the tar and then wash him with a mild shampoo. Never use turpentine or kerosene. These substances are irritating to the skin and toxic to your dog if he tries to lick them off.

Some dogs may need to be restrained or even (in worst cases) muzzled during the procedure. It's important to do whatever it takes, though, because nails that grow too long can split painfully. They can also break off, bleed, get caught in rugs or crate mesh, and cause great pain. If the nails aren't trimmed frequently enough, the vein within will get longer until it's impossible to cut the nail to a normal length. Long nails can even splay out the foot so badly it becomes deformed. No matter how distasteful the process is to you or your dog, you must trim his nails. If you can hear your dog's nails clicking on the floor, they are too long.

To begin trimming, take the dog's paw gently in hand and softly squeeze it to extend the nails. Clip the tip, but be careful to avoid the quick, the blood vessel that runs nearly to the end of the nail. You can't see it in dark-nailed dogs (like some black Labs), so you'll need to clip just a tiny bit at a time. However, if you look closely, you'll notice a small white spot at the tip of the nail. Stop there. This is the quick. The quick has both a nerve and blood supply; if you accidentally cut it, your dog will cry and perhaps bleed.

Always keep styptic powder on hand in case you cut into the quick. If you do accidentally clip a nail too short, apply styptic powder right away. The bleeding will stop immediately. If you don't happen to have styptic powder, any flour-based product (like cornstarch) will work.

Don't feel compelled to trim every nail if the procedure frightens your dog. Do just two or three at a time. However, don't allow your dog to "win" if he objects. If he protests and you quit, then he will be even more adamantly against it next time. You must finish on a successful note. Praise and a treat are great ways to make nail trimming a positive experience for your Lab.

EAR CARE

Ears need to be cleaned regularly, at least once a week. If your dog tends to have serious wax buildup or similar problems, clean them more often. Use a commercial, nonalcohol-based ear wash or a good herbal product with mullein to bring wax and dirt to the surface.

When cleaning the ears, just massage them gently. Avoid the urge to use a cotton swab—it's easy to go too far into the ear canal and damage it. A cotton ball is a better choice. Don't insert anything deeply into the ear, because you could damage the delicate tissues.

The dog's ear is L-shaped, so you can't get to the bottom of it anyway.

Because the ears are an extension of the skin, dogs with skin problems often tend to have ear problems as well, and vice versa. If your dog pulls away or resists having you examine his ear, assume that something is wrong.

Dark, gritty material in the ears may signal ear mites. You can't see mites without magnification, but an infected dog may scratch the hair off the back of his ears for relief. You can buy a commercial cleaner to get rid of them. Red, smelly, or inflamed ears indicate a bacterial or fungal infection, in which case you'll need to see your veterinarian.

EYE CARE

Cleaning and examining the eyes should be a regular part of grooming. If a slight irritation appears, you can apply a commercial nonmedicated eyewash. Gently clean away any discharge that has

Let the clear, clean eyes of your puppy be your barometer for how your Lab's eyes should look as he gets older.

gathered at the corners of the eye. If the discharge is yellow or green and the eye is swollen or red, the dog needs veterinary care immediately.

To examine your dog's eyes, simply stroke him gently on the head, pulling back the ears. The eyes will naturally open wider and come clearly into view. A healthy dog's eyes should be wide open and bright. The center should be clear and shining, with pupils that are the same size. (If they are of unequal size, a neurological problem could be present.) The whites of the eyes should be pure white with no redness. Older dogs may have a greenish tinge to their eyes, but this is a normal characteristic of aging and nothing to worry about. The tissue beneath the lower lids should be a healthy pink, although some animals have a dark tinge on the membrane.

DENTAL CARE

Good dental care includes examining and brushing your Lab's teeth on a daily basis.

Tooth brushing is an essential element of good grooming. The average adult dog has 42 teeth. (Puppies have only 28.) Every one of these teeth requires care. According to the American

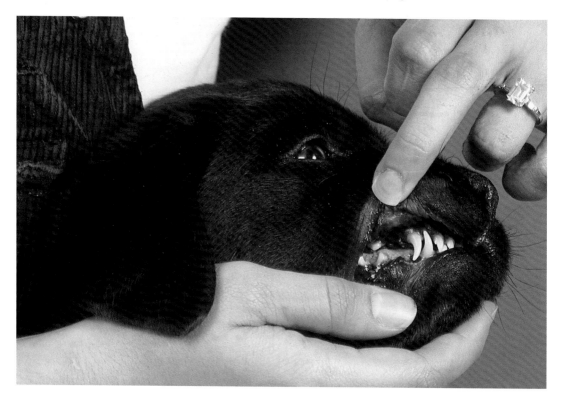

Anal Sacs

The anal sacs (often mistakenly called "glands") are two round organs located on each side of the anus (at the 4 and 8 o'clock positions). They exude powerful, bad-smelling secretions that are apparently used to give other dogs mating and territorial information. Every time the dog defecates, some of this material is deposited. Dogs can also empty their sacs when they are scared or overexcited. A few dogs, however, have difficulty expressing these sacs on their own. Some people recommend routinely emptying the anal sacs as a regular part of grooming, but this is not always a wise idea and can lead to more problems, like further infection.

Dogs of all breeds and of any age may encounter anal sac problems. Anal sacs can become infected with bacteria (anal sacculitis), become impacted or overfilled, which can lead to acute discomfort and infection, and develop tumors or foreign bodies.

Signs that your Labrador is encountering anal sac problems include:
- Scooting his rear end along the ground.
- Chewing or licking the tail base.
- Clamping the tail down over the anus.
- Reluctance to sit.
- Difficulty in passing feces.
- Redness or swelling in the area, perhaps even an open, draining sore.

Dogs with a history of anal sac problems may be candidates for having them surgically removed. Because your dog doesn't really "need" them, this is a pretty benign procedure, although you need to find a vet who is experienced with performing the operation. A careless mistake could injure the sphincter muscles.

Veterinary Dental Society (AVDS), about 80 percent of dogs have signs of dental disease by the time they are three years old; in fact, this is one of the most common health problem seen by veterinarians.

Like people, dogs can experience a buildup of plaque that combines with food particles and saliva and turns into tartar. Tartar actually builds up within a few hours after a meal! Bacteria buildup not only causes bad breath and threatens teeth; there's evidence that the infection can invade other parts of the dog's body and cause damage to the heart, liver, and kidneys. When food particles get trapped in the crevices of your dog's teeth, he can develop gingivitis, an inflammation of the gums. The main sign of gingivitis is bleeding and redness. Untreated gingivitis can lead to periodontal disease. Fortunately, the right chew toys, like Nylabones, can assist in promoting healthy teeth and gums.

Good dental care means brushing, and you should brush your dog's teeth every day. Nothing else works as well. The more often you brush your dog's teeth, the better his dental health will

be. If you don't brush your dog's teeth every day, do so as often as you can, beginning when your Labrador is a puppy. Your puppy may not look as if he needs his teeth brushed, but getting him used to the process early in his life will make things easier later. Don't wait until your dog is actually showing signs of dental disease, because it's too late at this point. Eight to 12 weeks old is not too early!

It's important to help your dog become gradually familiar with the process of brushing. To this end, select a rubber finger brush that slides over your forefinger. Don't worry about toothpaste yet—just massage with the finger brush. After a week or so of "pasteless brushing," add the toothpaste. Use a kind made just for dogs. (They come in a variety of flavors, including chicken, beef, mint, and peanut butter.) Dogs like meat-flavored toothpastes the best, of course, although people usually prefer mint, both for themselves and their dog. Never give your dog human toothpaste, though. Dogs swallow toothpaste, and human toothpaste, which is not meant to be swallowed, will irritate their stomachs.

When you get good at this, it will take less than 30 seconds for the actual brushing. You'll be doing your part to keep your dog's teeth clean and his mouth smelling fresh.

When you brush the teeth, examine the gums. They should be a clean, healthy pink. Gums that are dark red, pale, gray, or yellowish may signal a serious disease. Liver problems, infections, and anemia all reveal themselves in the gums.

Check your dog for the following signs of dental disease:
- Bleeding
- Tartar buildup
- Bad breath
- Reddened gums
- Difficulty chewing
- Change in eating habits
- Pawing at the mouth

Dental Visits

Just as you need to go to the dentist for an annual dental checkup and cleaning, so does your dog. When he reaches one year of age, have his teeth cleaned annually, and at six years, a twice yearly exam is best. The dental exam may include radiographs, because about 70 percent of the tooth is below the gumline.

Most dogs have their dental cleaning done under short-acting anesthesia. Your veterinarian will use special ultrasound equipment (plus the manual work) to remove plaque above and below the gumline. She will follow it up with polishing and fluoride treatment.

Doggie dental care rivals the human kind nowadays. Canine dentists can do implants, braces, root canals, bonding, and even whitening. However, if you don't hold up your end by brushing your dog's teeth, all that fancy work will go to waste.

Grooming time provides the perfect opportunity for you and your Lab to bond.

TRAINING AND BEHAVIOR
of Your Labrador Retriever

There is no excuse for not having a well-trained Labrador. Along with Golden Retrievers, Poodles, German Shepherds, and Border Collies, these super-trainable dogs excel at all aspects of training, from basic obedience to creative problem solving. But they don't train themselves. If your Labrador is not well trained, look no farther than the mirror.

Dogs live in the present tense. They don't think about the future, and they don't regret the past. This is an admirable living strategy, but it's also rather inflexible. It is up to us humans (who presumably can think about the future and past) to help our dogs learn to follow household rules.

It is also important to remember that Labradors are fairly slow to mature in comparison with some other breeds. Expect your Lab to be a happy, energetic puppy well after he is officially an "adult" at the age of one year. Many owners say that Labs don't fully mature until they are three years old—that's a long puppyhood!

SOCIALIZATION

Labradors are naturally very friendly dogs, and this is a trait you want to encourage as much as possible. When going out, take your dog everywhere, and have him meet people of different genders, ages, races, sizes, and dress and with all sorts of accoutrements, like canes, bikes, wheelchairs, skateboards, and grocery bags. I have even known dogs suspicious of people wearing hats, sunglasses, or overcoats. If your dog has problems with any of these things, obtain the assistance of friendly strangers by asking them to give your dog a small treat.

If your new Labrador is a puppy, restrict the number of visits with other dogs until he has had his second set of shots. That doesn't mean you shouldn't take him out at all, but you should limit his contacts with other dogs. Many contagious diseases are lurking around. Be particularly careful when going for a walk in the park, because some people do not clean up after their dogs, and many viral diseases are carried in feces. (This is a good reason to check your own shoes when returning from a walk—you may have stepped in something unpleasant yourself.)

HOUSETRAINING

Puppies will have accidents, just as kids do. Humans are supposed to be smarter than dogs, but many children are often not toilet trained until the age of three—yet some owners expect their puppy to be perfect at four months! If you change those unrealistic expectations, you'll save yourself a lot of grief.

If you're oblivious to what's going on until your puppy actually starts eliminating, don't panic. It's not the end of the world. If you start screaming, you'll convince your dog that he has done something awful (not that eliminating in the house is awful, but that eliminating altogether is awful). Because your Labrador can't stop eliminating, he'll start hiding it. The key is to act calmly and to promptly teach the puppy the nuanced lesson that eliminating outside is award winning; eliminating inside is not.

Keys to Successful Housetraining

The keys to successful housetraining include:

- Crate
- Reward
- Attention
- Patience
- Scheduling

Although Labradors are naturally friendly dogs, it's still important to socialize them from an early age.

Crate

If your dog accepts his crate as his sleeping den, he will be less likely to use it as a toilet. Dogs simply don't like to eliminate where they sleep. Of course, you can't keep your dog in a crate longer than his bowels and bladder can stand! Remember that puppies have tiny bladders, and their sphincters are insufficiently developed to hold waste for a long period of time. You should never keep a puppy in a crate for more than two hours except at night, when he is supposed to be sleeping anyway. Confining a dog for long periods in a crate is extremely detrimental to his physical and emotional health. Sooner or later, he will start eliminating in the crate out of necessity—and if he doesn't, he may be well on his way to developing bladder stones.

Reward

Always reward your puppy, or for that matter, an untrained older dog, with praise or a treat when he eliminates outdoors. If he responds to praise, that's best. Make the praise overwhelming—jump for joy! Let him know that you are thrilled with his behavior. Most Labradors are truly anxious to please you. Another treasured reward is a walk. Some people take their dog out, let him eliminate, and then immediately bring him back inside. As a result, the message he is getting is that as soon as he eliminates, it's time to go back in the house. This may cause him to try to hold it as long as possible, potentially resulting in accidents indoors.

As an alternative, give your dog a walk or a play session as soon as he's successful. If you do take him out for a long walk and don't get a result, try bringing him indoors and then *immediately* taking him out again. He may have forgotten his duties during the excitement of the walk and won't remember until he's inside again. Most importantly, never punish your dog for making a mistake. Don't yell at him, strike him, or rub his nose in his mistake. These practices are cruel and ineffective.

Attention

Your dog will give you signals that he needs to go out, but it's up to you to figure out what they are. Sometimes, a dog will do something refreshingly obvious like actually going to the door. But don't expect that, at least not at first. It's more likely that your dog

Puppy Rules

Don't allow a little puppy to get away with something you wouldn't enjoy with an adult dog. It's cute when puppies jump in your lap, but when your 80-pound adult hurls himself onto frail old Aunt Yvette, nobody is going to be laughing.

In Praise of Labs

While all dogs enjoy praise, Labs are one of the few breeds that respond best to low-key, rather restrained praise, especially when working on important matters such as retrieving. Overpraising your Lab can actually cause him to lose his concentration, which will then slow down the whole training process.

will give you subtle signs that he has to go, like licking his lips, circling, looking puzzled, or if you're really lucky, actually whining. The instant you notice these signals, grab the leash and take him out. Don't simply put the dog out and hope all will be well. Go out with him so that you can praise his success.

Patience

You wouldn't expect to toilet train a child in a week, so don't expect your Labrador to be reliable after only a few days, either. He is a baby with weak sphincter muscles and a small bladder. By properly using the crate, watching your dog like a hawk, and keeping to a schedule, you'll encourage the proper response from him. But a puppy will inevitably make some mistakes. If you don't find these mistakes until after the fact, simply clean them up without comment. If you catch the puppy in the act, scoop him up, tuck his tail between his legs (this helps prevent "spillage"), and say, "Out!" or "Quick!" Don't say, "No!" "No" is a negative word, and your puppy may think that eliminating is wrong, no matter where he does it. If he gets that idea, he'll start hiding it from you.

Schedule

Dogs not only like routine, but it's also good for them. Put your puppy on a regular feeding and elimination schedule as soon as possible. The more regular the schedule, the easier it will be to housetrain your dog. This may mean you will have to take some time off from work or hire a puppy sitter during the housetraining process, which usually takes about two weeks if you do everything right. This may seem extreme, but believe me, it makes all the difference. Your puppy usually needs to eliminate after naps, after meals, after playtime, first thing in the morning, and last thing at night. You'll probably have better luck if you give your puppy his last meal around six o'clock in the evening. If you feed him any later than that, you'll be getting up later that night to take him out.

Different dogs have different schedules. You may have one who needs to go out when you're eating, when you are taking a shower, when you're on a conference call, or during the most thrilling moments of your favorite television show. However, this is all part of the wonder of owning a Labrador!

Establishing a Schedule

Dog behaviorist Laura Hussey gives a sample schedule for housetraining a young dog. It is useful not only for housetraining but also for elementary leash walking.

- 5:30 a.m.—Wake up, immediately go outside to potty.
- 5:40-6:00 a.m.—Cuddling/handling time. Socialize the dog to having paws handled, nails trimmed, ears cleaned.
- 6:00 a.m.—Breakfast.
- 6:15-6:30 a.m.—Playtime and more handling.
- 6:30 a.m.—Potty trip. (At this age, your puppy will probably have to go within 20 minutes of eating.)
- 6:40-7:00 a.m.—Short walk on leash to get used to the neighborhood, learn to walk nicely on leash
- 7:00-7:30 a.m.—Go in crate with a chew toy while you get ready for the day.
- 7:30 a.m.—Outside for potty trip.
- 8:00-12:00 noon—Naptime in crate.

You can feed a puppy a midday meal if your schedule allows, in which case you would start the timing above when the dog wakes up—that is, go outside immediately, followed by some handling, then food, etc.

Repeat again in the evening for an evening meal, followed perhaps by longer playtime. Remember that young dogs will often have to relieve themselves when they get excited, such as during active play.

When Accidents Occur

If your puppy does have an accident on the carpet, dilute the spot with a dampened cloth. Then, clean the area with a bacteria/enzyme digester available at your local pet supply, grocery, or hardware store. These get rid of both the stain and the smell. The latter is very important; even if you can't smell the urine, your dog can, and he will only be encouraged to use the spot again. For best results, make sure you use enough of the product to penetrate both the

Exercise needs to be a part of your Lab's daily routine—for his lifetime!

The Glories of the Doggie Door

The doggie door is a wonderful invention! With a doggie door, your Labrador is ruler of the house and backyard and has control of his environment. This alone will help make him feel happy and secure.

Most dogs learn to use a pet door with ease. To make it as simple as possible, though, you may wish to leave off the flap at first. Get one person to stand on one side of the door and call the Lab. Reward him with praise or a treat when he crosses though. Do this a few times and he'll get the idea. Leave the flap off until you feel he's comfortable and secure with the concept. Then, install the flap and repeat the exercise. You may have to hold it aside first. And yes, you may have to go through it yourself!

carpet and the pad underneath. Leave it on for the required length of time. Enzyme digesters work very well, but they are not quick fixes. After you put down the solution, cover the area with plastic and step on it a few times to ensure the spot is well saturated. Keep the plastic in place so the digester doesn't dry out. (Never use an ammonia product to clean up dog urine. It smells like urine to dogs and will only encourage them to use that spot again.)

BASIC COMMANDS

Labradors are among the most highly trainable of dog breeds. They can learn in ten minutes what it takes many breeds weeks or months to figure out. However, Labradors are still dogs, and for successful training, your best bet is to rely on the essentials: timing, rewards, and consistency. Timing refers to when you train, how often you train, and how quickly you respond to your dog's errors or successes. Rewards can include treats, praise, or petting. Consistency means that you have a plan and you stick with it.

When you train your Labrador, it's important to work in a controlled, quiet environment. As the dog becomes more proficient, you can increase the level of distraction, perhaps finishing up in the dog park. It's also important to keep commands as simple as possible, preferably strong, one-syllable words. Speak firmly but not angrily so that your dog will know you mean business. Dogs read your tone, body language, and attitude, as well as your words.

Good training doesn't have to mean your dog is ready for high-level obedience work, though. It does mean, at minimum, that you should have a well-mannered house dog. The well-mannered house dog will greet visitors politely, allow himself to be petted without running away or snarling, remove himself from the sofa when asked, walk quietly on a leash, get into the bathtub without a fuss, allow his nails to be clipped without having a hissy fit, ride well in the car, and not whine when restricted to another part of the house.

Begin training with a handful of tiny treats, and let the dog know you have them. That's the best way to get his attention, and getting his attention is the first step in training. When he looks at you, reward him. Soon he will get the idea that paying close attention is a good way to get fed.

Watch Me

This is the basic focus command. If your dog isn't paying any attention to you, he won't be able to learn anything. Help him focus by using positive reinforcements and treats. This doesn't mean that you should give your dog food every time he looks at you. It means that he should always consider it as a viable possibility. Once he learns that "watch me!" brings praise or even a reward, he'll be anxious to learn what you have to say next.

To teach your Lab to sit, hold a treat just above his nose while saying, "Sit."

To teach watch me, say the words and hold a treat near your face. If your Labrador doesn't see the treat at first, you may have to start to lower it toward his field of vision. He'll catch on soon.

The number of times you do anything should depend on the age, training, and maturity of your Labrador. Stop while he is still having fun! Usually a minute or two is long enough.

Sit

Although sit is not really a critical command, dogs learn it easily, and it's fun to teach. You will both feel as if you have accomplished something. People who work retrievers in hunting or field trials say that the soft, sibilant "s" of sit makes the word clearly understandable even in the softest whisper. (After all, you don't want to scare the birds away!)

To teach him to sit, take a tasty morsel and hold it just above the dog's nose. Say, "Sit" in a gentle, encouraging way, and move the treat back over the dog's head. He will sit naturally. Don't attempt to push down on his hindquarters. This use of force is unnatural and can even be damaging to a Labrador. The very instant that he sits, reward him. Say something like "good!" or "yippee!" in a happy tone of voice, or use a clicker or even a gesture to mark the behavior. Repeat the exercise. Some dogs learn this almost at once, but with others, it may take as many as 30 repetitions.

Teach stay by saying the word and then gradually and slowly retreating.

Stay

Although some people teach the stay as a separate command, I prefer to use the sit, which means that my dog should sit until I say, "Okay!" I believe that teaching the stay as a separate command is confusing to dogs, because you're not asking them to do anything new—you're just asking them to keep doing what you have already asked them to do. However, other people believe that saying, "Stay" signals to the dog early that he'll be sitting for quite some time. At any rate, never ask your dog to sit-stay for more than a few seconds when you are starting out. You want to make success easy for him.

Teach stay by saying the word and gradually and slowly retreating. Reward him for remaining in one place.

Again, quit while the training is still fun. The length of time you teach this command depends on your individual dog, but five minutes is usually long enough.

Come

The come command is one of the most critical commands of all, because it can save your dog's life. Most dogs pick this command up naturally, but it's important for them to have some formal schooling as well.

After your dog learns to sit and stay, slowly move away from him. Twenty feet is far enough. Call him, clapping your hands if necessary to get his attention. If you have to, start walking away from him. Don't ever chase him, though, because that will encourage him to run in the opposite direction. If he still won't come on command, you may have to attach a long lead line and start gently drawing him toward you using treats.

Behaviorist Laura Hussey advises, "If there is something your dog doesn't like, such as having a bath or getting his nails trimmed, go and get the dog for that activity rather than calling him to you. The rationale behind this tip is that you want to have a dog who enthusiastically comes running when you call, and the best way to ensure that is to make sure that every time you call, a happy experience awaits your dog. If he learns that sometimes when he comes you give him a bath or trim his nails, he will be much less willing to come. Instead, when you need the dog for one of those unpleasant tasks, go to the dog without calling his name and lead him back with you."

Leave It

Young dogs are always getting into trash, diapers, and expensive shoes. Start teaching your Lab to drop such objects by waiting until he is chewing on something he really doesn't care that much about. (It should also be one that's not important to you, either.) As he's chewing, say, "Leave it!" Offer him a tasty treat in exchange, something he likes better than whatever it is he has. Bacon and liver treats, for example, are great favorites. Praise him when he accepts the exchange.

In real life, you'll be most likely to use this command when the dog has gotten into something really irresistible, like a deer carcass, so your established reward needs to be very powerful. Of course, you probably won't have any bacon on hand when the infraction occurs, but it's okay to cheat once in a while. Afterward, practice leave it several more times with your accustomed treat and plenty of praise.

Down

While the dog is sitting, hold the treat in front and gradually lower it to the ground between his front legs. The Labrador should lie down as well. Some dogs resist this movement because it puts them in a vulnerable position. However, if your dog has confidence in your leadership, you should be able to teach this command.

In formal obedience classes, your Labrador may learn a long down-stay, which usually lasts for several minutes. This command is simply a combination of down and stay.

Heel (Walk by Your Side)

Your Labrador should be responding to the come command before you start teaching him to heel, which means to walk nicely on a lead at your heel. Your leash is your dog's best friend. Don't think of the leash as a restraining device; think of it as a way to stay

"Gentle" Feeding

If your dog is a grabber and attempts to snatch food from you, avoid the problem by just dropping the food on the floor. Don't attempt to correct this habit while trying to teach him to sit— it will really confuse him. Work on the grabbing issue separately by holding the treat firmly in your fist and murmuring, "Gentle, gentle" as your dog attempts to extract it.

close to your dog. Soon your Labrador will look forward to the sight of the leash because it means it's time for a walk! However, Labradors are very strong dogs, and they can be pullers. Thus, it is doubly important for your dog to learn to walk calmly and pleasantly on a leash with you in control. If you don't teach your dog proper leash behavior very early, you're in for a difficult time.

When teaching your Labrador to heel, don't pull or jerk on the leash. Only use it to keep him from going in the other direction. If your Labrador starts to pull, turn the other way without a word. Keep repeating this exercise. This will focus his attention on you. Because no one likes to be pulled, he'll start paying attention and trying to anticipate your moves. Say, "Heel" in a quiet, firm voice as you turn. Don't go around aimlessly turning, however, just in order to confuse your dog. Turn only in response to his pulling against you. (When your dog becomes more adept at heeling, you can practice more complicated patterns.)

Labradors are one of the most highly trainable dog breeds.

If you are going to go hunting with your Labrador, you will teach the dog to heel on the opposite side that you carry a gun. Otherwise (and in obedience work) it's traditional to have the dog heel on the left side. Start walking, and hold a treat to his nose. The dog will naturally follow. Use a leash to continue to change directions, and stop frequently. Very soon, your Labrador will be heeling naturally.

FORMAL TRAINING

It doesn't hurt to reinforce what you've learned at home by taking your Labrador to formal obedience classes. Obedience classes also double as socialization events, so you'll really be getting twice as much for your money. Before you go, know exactly what you are looking for. Some classes focus on household manners and basic commands, while others prepare you for formal obedience work. Choose the class and the teacher that best fits your needs. It

may be worthwhile to visit the class first and observe the teacher in action. Avoid any teacher who relies on force or harsh methods.

The heel command will teach your Lab how to walk nicely on a lead at your heel.

The most advanced level of trainer is probably someone who has been certified by the Animal Behavior Society. Most of these people are veterinarians or Ph.D.s, and there are fewer than 50 of them in the entire world. Someone with a graduate degree in animal behavior may use the title "animal behaviorist." Trainers without the degree but with the experience may call themselves "behavior consultants" or "behavior counselors."

More important than the degree, though, is the style of the trainer. Don't be afraid to shop around and find someone whose style "clicks" with your dog (even if she doesn't use a clicker). Look for an instructor who is willing to listen to you and help you achieve the goals you have set for yourself and your dog.

PROBLEM BEHAVIORS

Dogs don't have a sense of morality. They don't see ripping apart a pillow, biting a child, urinating in the house, or barking all day as "wrong." They also don't look at obeying their owners, heeling on a lead, or behaving nicely around other dogs and people as "right." They are free of a sense of guilt. This lighthearted, pleasant attitude makes dogs really easy to train, actually. You don't have to waste

Using a Whistle

Many people like to train their Labrador Retrievers using a whistle, which is especially handy if you plan to be out in the woods and fields all day. In conventional "retriever vocabulary," one sharp whistle means, "Stop where you are and wait for more orders," while four or five short, quick blasts means, "Come right away." Of course, dogs aren't born knowing this language, any more than people are born knowing English or French. At any rate, you can practice using the voice command and follow up with the whistle.

time instilling a moral code in dogs. All you need to do is show them what works best for them. Problems arise when dogs discover this on their own; they have already decided what works best, and you haven't been on the ball to show them differently. Almost every single problem a dog presents is traceable to ignorance, neglect, or mistakes in training on the part of the person who owns him.

Remember that while I'm going to give you some advice for handling common canine problem behaviors, you may not be able to solve every problem yourself. If what you're doing (or what I suggest that you do) doesn't bring results, it's time to try a different method, like consulting a dog behaviorist.

We humans are odd creatures who tend to try doing the same things over and over again, even though our experience has shown that what we're doing doesn't work. Dog training and solving problem behaviors are customized enterprises. What works well for one dog or owner might fall flat with another, and what worked yesterday may fail today. That's why it helps to be creative. Think like a dog; this simple trick is often all you need to envision a problem in a new way.

Nipping

Puppy nipping is a form of play. It does *not* usually result from teething, as teething is more likely to produce chewing and gnawing than nipping. Rest assured, though—nipping is normal in puppies. However, if unrestrained, it can lead to painful bites.

Solution

To reduce the amount of nipping, make sure your dog has opportunities for non-damaging play: retrieving, lots of walks and runs, swimming, and learning tricks. Many of these activities exercise the Lab's mind as well as his body.

Despite your best efforts, however, your puppy may still nip at you. The incidence of nipping is usually lessened, though, if you have a puppy who was allowed to remain with his litter until he was eight or nine weeks old. Until this point, puppies learn the invaluable skill of bite inhibition. They learn when playing with other puppies that an uninhibited bite causes their littermates to cry and scramble away—playtime over. Soon, the puppies learn to control the force of the bite.

Even though your puppy is no longer with his litter, you can continue to teach bite inhibition at home. Do not allow a hard nip to go unnoticed. (He'll bite harder next time if you do.) He needs to know that this behavior is unacceptable. It's easy to teach him this: At the first nip, yip like a wounded puppy and cease interaction if he doesn't stop. Just walk away. It's important to do this even if the nip doesn't hurt that much. Your puppy will consequently learn that nipping people results in a loss of playtime.

Labs are mouthy dogs, and the lesson you want yours to learn is that all mouthing is painful to humans. Remember that your puppy is trying to play with you—it's up to you to teach him how to do it correctly.

Ignore Bad Behavior

Many problem behaviors originate from a dog's bid for attention. The dog acts "badly," and he consequently receives attention for that undesirable attention. Ideally, then, you want to teach your dog an alternative behavior and give him attention for performing the alternative.

Chewing

Chewing is the Labrador's specialty. Puppies discover the world by chewing on it, and Labradors are among the most famous chewers of all. A puppy has no way of knowing what is allowed to be chewed and what isn't. Until he is old enough to discriminate, you must supervise him every waking hour.

Solution

If you catch your Labrador in the act of chewing, cry, "No chew!" and give him something else to work on. Because dogs must chew, give him something appropriate to chew on instead, such as a Nylabone. Rotate his chew toys so that he doesn't lose interest in them. While chewing is a natural way to explore the environment (and older puppies may chew to use up some of their relentless energy), adult dogs may chew out of anxiety, boredom, or fear. However, some Labradors, even as they grow to adulthood, will continue to chew just because they enjoy it. It's their nature and is probably their biggest "fault" as far as their owners are concerned.

To prevent your Labrador from chewing on inappropriate

objects, supervise him when you're home, and crate or confine him with appropriate chews when you have to leave the home. If your dog has the run of the house, you'll need to remove any valuables (which may include the rug).

You can separate normal chewing from stress chewing by conducting this simple test. If the dog chews in your presence, it's probably normal behavior that you need only redirect. If he chews only while you're away, it's anxiety related. If you feel the chewing is related to anxiety, don't crate your Labrador; you'll only exacerbate the problem. In this case, you'll need to work on the cause of the problem rather than its effect. (For more information, see section on separation anxiety.)

If your Labrador tends to chew your favorite items, try substituting a safe, appropriate chew toy instead.

Rough Play

Everything you do with your Labrador puppy teaches him something. When you play roughly with him, you're teaching him to play roughly with you. If you use your hands as toys, don't be surprised when he bites them. In the same way, if your puppy steals your sock and you chase him, you're reinforcing the fact that stealing stuff is a great way for him to get your attention. (If he does take something, you'll have better luck getting it back if you get him to chase you. Labradors can run faster than people.)

Solution

If your Lab plays too roughly, end the game. Labs are smart enough to know that they'll need to moderate their behavior if they want to keep having fun!

With some dogs, games of rough play can result in aggressive behavior. If you have a dog who seems to be vying with you for dominance, avoid games of tug-of-war and play fighting.

Dogs and Babies

Adding a baby to your household is a thrilling event for you but a stressful one for your dog. To make the transition as easy as possible, try to prepare your Labrador in advance. Realistically, you know that a new baby will take up a lot of your time and that in all likelihood, your precious Lab will not receive all the attention he's been accustomed to. It might be hard now, but start cutting your interactions with your dog before the baby arrives. That way he won't associate your withdrawn attention with the arrival of a new infant. If there is someone else in the house who can give the dog extra attention and who won't be so engrossed with the new baby (perhaps an older child), this might be a good time to start redirecting the dog's focus to that person. Have the family member start walking, feeding, and playing more with the dog.

Make sure your pet is well trained and responds to basic commands such as sit and stay. He should be trained not to jump onto the couch with you unless specifically invited to do so. If necessary, enroll him in a training class. Another way to prepare for the baby's arrival is to get your Lab a wellness check before the baby arrives. Keep his nails clipped to reduce the possibility of scratching. Also, if you have friends or neighbors with babies, ask them to bring them over so that the Lab doesn't find your own new child a completely alien creature. If he reacts positively, give him a special treat.

While bringing a baby home is a thrilling time, for a dog it can be confusing as well. New sounds, new sights, and most of all, new smells, are in the air. Planning is the key. You can help your dog ease the transition by letting him become familiar with the smell of baby lotion, dirty diapers, and even an article of clothing the baby has worn before actually meeting the child. There is even a CD available that helps a dog become accustomed to the various noises emitted by a baby, including grunting, breathing, screaming, wailing, and squeaking.

Another option that reduces canine stress is a product that releases dog-appeasing pheromones. The pheromones in question are the ones produced by a lactating mother dog. This easy to use over-the-counter remedy plugs into an electrical outlet and has an instant calming effect on many dogs—with no side effects.

If you've already selected a baby name, use it a lot in front of the dog. That way, the baby won't seem like such a stranger. After the baby is born but before you bring her home, get someone to bring home a blanket that's been used. That may help the dog become accustomed to the specific scent of the baby. Some experts advise you to place your dog with a neighbor for a few hours after the baby comes home. That way, the presence of the child will already be an established fact.

When you do greet your dog, have some treats at hand and remain calm. As he meets the baby, reward him when he behaves appropriately. And of course, always supervise. To keep things on an even keel, try to maintain as regular a schedule as you can. Dogs and babies both appreciate that!

Digging

Digging is a natural activity for dogs. They dig to find cool places to rest in the summer, to hunt for little critters in the ground, to prepare a nest, and just for something to do when they're bored. Unfortunately, this natural behavior can turn your lawn into a minefield.

Solution

You have several approaches when it comes to digging, all of which involve management. First, you can encourage your dog to dig where you want him to by supplying him with an "earthbox,"

Exercise and Problem Behaviors

Many problem behaviors (chewing, barking, digging, running away) occur simply because the dog is bored. A little exercise can go a long way toward reducing or even eliminating inappropriate behavior. Frequent exercise at a level suitable for your dog's condition is an excellent way not only to prevent problems but also to solidify the bond between you.

Let common sense be your guide. Hold off on exercise until at least an hour after the dog has consumed a large meal. Choose areas with soft grass or dirt to exercise; hard or slippery places can damage paw pads or lead to injury. Avoid exercising your cold-loving Lab on very hot days to avoid heatstroke, and always provide him with plenty of cool water. Jumping and twisting exercise is hard on the back and joints, so avoid these kinds of activities if you have an older dog, a puppy, or any dog whose health is in question. You'll soon discover the enormous mental and physical benefits of exercise for both of you!

which is simply a child's sandbox filled with attractive, soft, diggable earth or play sand. You can encourage him to dig in it by hiding one of his more precious toys there. You can also restrict your dog's access to valuable real estate with a fence. If this is not practical, simply watch him like a hawk and put him in the earthbox, perhaps with a great toy anchored to it to encourage his presence. However, you should never punish your dog for doing what comes naturally.

If your Labrador digs inside the house, he may be looking for mice or other home invaders. It's also common for dogs to dig at new carpeting. The new material hasn't yet absorbed the familiar odors of the house, and your dog might dig at it to find out just what this strange new stuff is made of. You'll need to keep your dog separated from the new material until the carpet has absorbed familiar household odors. Some kinds of digging is nesting behavior, too. If associated with other aberrant behavior, it might be an emotional problem. Usually, though, digging is just normal behavior.

Jumping Up

Many dogs are filled with delight at the prospect of visiting family and friends, and they may jump on guests as soon as they walk in the door. In these cases, the dog is simply trying to make contact with them by jumping up, a behavior you may have permitted with your dog when he was a cute, tiny little puppy. You may have even helped him reach your face and encouraged him to lick and kiss you. Now that he's a great big dog, though, suddenly his leaping up to overwhelm you with his kisses isn't so cute anymore. If your Lab goes wild when visitors come, you can desensitize him to their presence.

Solution

Dog behaviorist Laura Hussey explains that some people have taught their dogs that the ringing of the doorbell is a cue for picking up a big chewy toy and carrying it around. When they do that, they get petted. Other dogs are taught that the ringing of the doorbell is a cue to sit in a particular place away from the door. You can practice either one of these exercises with the help of a willing participant who pretends to be a visitor. A neighborhood teen might be willing to help out, or maybe you have a friend or family member (not from your own household) who could work with you. If you can find a willing volunteer, arrange for her to come to your house and knock on the door or ring the doorbell at a prearranged time. In the meantime, you should have some good treats handy, as well as your dog's favorite toy. The purpose of the toy is to have something to stuff in your Lab's mouth to curb his barking. This does help with certain dogs, so it doesn't hurt to give it a try with yours.

Labs who have been taught to sit in order to receive attention, food, or other rewards will not jump up on people unless asked.

Hussey suggests the following steps:

1. When the doorbell rings, communicate to your dog that you will do the greeting by telling him in a firm but pleasant voice to sit. If he complies, give him a treat and open the door. You will have instructed your visitor ahead of time to cross her arms and turn her back to the dog if he jumps up but to pet him politely if he sits.

2. If your dog jumps up when the visitor comes in, the visitor should immediately use her body language to communicate that this is not acceptable by crossing her arms and turning her back. In the meantime, you should say, "Fido, sit." If the dog complies, your visitor should immediately turn around and politely pet the dog. Instruct the visitor to talk calmly to the dog in a soothing, lower-pitched voice, not in a high-pitched, excited voice that may get the dog more excited.

3. If your dog is showing improved

Stay Calm

Dogs are masters at sensing our moods, and our moods change when we are getting ready to leave the house. This change can trigger anxiety in a dog who doesn't like being alone. Establishing a calm routine—like putting your dog in his crate with a favorite toy or treat— and making your comings and goings as calm as possible can help your dog feel like it's no big deal that you're gone.

behavior, cut the visit short. Send the visitor away and tell your dog what a great job he did. Then, plan for practice, practice, and more practice. Ask your visitor to return in an hour or two to repeat the exercise. Repeat no more than four to five times. The key at this stage is not to let your dog practice the unacceptable behavior, only the improved behavior. This means that if you get a real visitor who won't be willing to go through some of the same steps you've been practicing, you should put your dog in another room or behind a baby gate before opening the door.

Separation Anxiety

Separation anxiety is one of the most common problem behaviors seen in dogs. A dog with this problem will become highly distressed when he senses you are about to leave home. When left alone, he may bark, howl, urinate, defecate, salivate, or destroy the house. He may also react with extreme joy when you return.

According to one estimate, 14 percent of dogs in the United States suffer from separation anxiety. Dogs are social beings who were never meant to spend hour after hour away from kith and kin. In fact, they need at least one hour, preferably two, of close human companionship a day to be happy and healthy. Walking, grooming, training, playing, and cuddling all count toward together time. Remember that although your dog may not be the center of your life, you are certainly the center of his. A lonely dog can become stressed, despondent, and destructive. While some dogs seem to manage well enough by themselves, most dogs need companionship—preferably yours. If that is not possible, adding another dog (or even a cat) to the family can soothe anxious moments. Dogs from shelters who have experienced abandonment suffer from separation anxiety the most.

Drug therapy is a new and very promising treatment for severe separation anxiety in dogs. However, before medicating your pet, see what behavior modifications you can make in your own lifestyle. Fortunately, neither you nor your dog has to continue suffering from separation anxiety. Treatment, both medical and behavioral, is available.

Solution

The following are various ways that you can help alleviate your Labrador's separation anxiety:

- **Crate Your Dog.** Crating may help create a sense of security for your dog, and even if it doesn't, he won't be chewing the furniture while he's confined. It's not safe to leave a puppy less than four months of age alone free in the house anyway; he simply does not have the psychological maturity to keep from ripping things into shreds. Don't leave him in the crate for more than four hours at the most, however. He needs both mental and physical stimulation he can't get in a crate. The condition of some dogs may worsen when crated.

- **Desensitize the Dog.** Start desensitizing your dog gradually to being left alone. Of course you can't take your dog with you to the opera, but it is not unreasonable to expect to be able to leave him alone for a few hours without returning to a war zone. One way you can do this is by getting him used to being on his own, even when you are at home. To accomplish this, discourage him from following you around the house, and give him his own chores to do (like chewing a bone). This doesn't mean you should ignore him; the goal is to build up his confidence and perception that he's a part of your life, even though you are not paying exclusive attention to him.

Another way you can desensitize your dog to being left alone is to prepare to leave the house without actually doing so. Jiggle the doorknob and jangle your keys. Do this several times a day, and soon your Labrador won't necessarily associate you getting out your purse with him being left alone.

When you do leave the house, don't make a big to-do about either departing or returning. Pay no attention to your dog for about 15 minutes or so before you leave. This means you should avoid even looking him, strange as it sounds, because this will actually have a calming effect on him. Looking at him raises his expectations and can make him nervous. You should only leave your Labrador unsupervised for gradually lengthened time periods. Get him used to the idea of you being gone. At first, leave and come back within a minute or two. Give him a toy as you depart, and collect it upon your

Dogs can learn that your leaving isn't anything to get upset about; in fact, it's an opportunity for a nice nap.

return. Soon, he'll understand that you'll always return, and he won't become destructive, at least not from separation anxiety. (That doesn't mean he won't get bored, however.) Most people make the mistake of not being gradual enough in their separation training. If your dog behaves well for one hour alone, do not assume he can be safely left for eight hours. Increase his periods alone by only fifteen minutes each time.

You can leave the radio or television on while you're gone. Studies show that classical music, for example, has a calming effect on dogs. You can also call your dog on the phone and leave him a nice message on the answering machine. Theoretically, the sound of your voice is supposed to have a calming effect on him.

For dogs who need extra exercise, hiring a professional dog walker who can spend some extra time with them is a worthwhile investment.

• **Don't Overstimulate the Dog.** This means you shouldn't soak him in attention when you're home and then suddenly leave. The contrast will be too much for him to bear. Sometimes it works better to be rather distant with a dog who is suffering from separation anxiety until he improves. This seems contradictory to the hour or so of attention I suggest giving him, and it may be. A lot depends on the individual dog.

• **Find a Pet Sitter or Dog Walker.** If you must be away from home for an extended period of time, hire someone trustworthy to entertain your dog. This gives him something to look forward to. When you return, you'll find a much quieter, happier dog. This does not have to be an expensive proposition. A responsible neighbor child might be happy to walk your dog for a nominal fee.

• **Get Another Dog or Cat.** Dogs are pack animals. Even though we have successfully bred them for thousands of years to think of us as their pack, there's no substitute for the real thing. Dogs interact naturally with each other, and just being in the company of their own kind may calm them down. (After all, the other dog won't make him sit or tell him to fetch. They'll just run around and be doggy together.) Your new dog doesn't have to be another Labrador; however, it usually works best if both dogs are approximately the same size. If two dogs are too much for you or are forbidden by the landlord, consider getting a cat. Even a cat who steadfastly ignores a dog will draw his attention.

- **Seek Professional Help and/or Medication.** Along with behavior modification, new medications are available. Some people object on principle to medicating their dogs. Although I empathize with those who want to treat their dogs naturally, there are times when modern pharmacology is the best answer. Consult with your veterinarian to see what, if any, medications are right for your Labrador.

About Biters

Male dogs are six times more likely to bite than females, and sexually intact dogs are 2.6 times more likely to bite than neutered dogs.

Aggression

Dog bites have reached epidemic proportions; every year in the United States, 4.7 million people are bitten by dogs, about 500,000 of them seriously enough to need medical attention. About ten people are killed by dogs every year, and most of the victims are children. While Labradors are renowned and bred for their generally upbeat, gentle temperaments, ill-bred and badly-trained Labs can and do bite. In fact, this sad trend seems to be on the upswing.

Almost all human-directed aggression is caused by stress. Exceptions are trained attack dogs and dogs who perceive a target as a prey animal. Because Labradors are not used as attack dogs, nor do they usually have a strong prey drive, you can assume that stress of some kind is at the root of the problem.

Physical causes should be considered first. If your dog becomes aggressive, he may be ill. Both arthritis and dental pain can turn a previously benign dog into a snappish one. Loss of vision and hearing will make him easily startled and confuse him. A dog with lessened mobility due to disease or age will feel unable to flee from a stressful situation and may feel he has no recourse other than to attack. Certain diseases also place stress on the nervous system. Psychological stress, brought on by something like moving, having a new baby, or bringing a new dog into the house, may also produce stress, especially if the dog feels he is being replaced by a more dominant animal or one who is receiving all of the attention.

Solution

If your Lab has shown aggression toward human beings, it's time to get professional help. Do not try to do this yourself—you will only make the problem worse. Your trainer should be someone experienced and skilled in dealing with aggressive dogs. Many obedience trainers are not.

Dog-Dog Aggression

While Labradors are normally the most peaceful of dogs, feuding can erupt among them. Many quarrels among dogs result from a struggle for top-dog status. Not every group of dogs has a top dog, however. Those who do have a top dog choose the alpha on the basis of many factors, including seniority in the home, age, sex, size, and so on. Human beings are constantly upsetting the "pack order" by adding new canine and human members to the pack. When that happens, there may be some disruption.

Solution

It's best to make introductions between dogs on neutral territory. Things can be tough, however, when a new dog shows up without having been properly socialized. I can't stress enough how important it is that you allow the dogs to settle who the top dog is among themselves. If you just support their decision, you'll put an end to most of the bickering. Let the top dog get the first pets, first greetings, and first food rights. Don't try to make things equal. Life isn't like that anyway. It shouldn't really matter to you who the top dog is. You're the boss of all of them!

If you have the opportunity to assess both the resident dog's personality as well as that of the newcomer, you'll find yourself ahead of the game. Older dogs may not appreciate the antics of a young puppy, for example. And sometimes, trouble erupts when the young puppy enters adolescence and makes a try for the top-dog position. To deal with this situation, keep your leadership but let the dogs work things out for themselves unless you feel the puppy is in real danger. When you are walking your Labrador and meet another dog, it's important to keep calm and make sure the leash is reasonably loose. If you tighten the leash, your tension will be felt by the dog, who in turn will become tense. Train your Lab to walk quietly at heel, or even ask him to sit/stay when a strange dog passes by.

Give him a small treat to reward him for his good behavior.

House Soiling

Sometimes it may appear that your older dog has forgotten he's been housetrained. Don't assume the dog is angry with you, though. Like aggression, house soiling is often brought about by physical problems or stress. Medical problems leading to house soiling include colitis, anal sac disease, hormone-responsive incontinence, inflammatory bowel disease, diabetes, bladder problems, inflammation of the prostate, Cushing's disease, or problems with the liver or kidney. Older animals who suffer from arthritis or other movement-inhibiting conditions are less likely to want to make the painful trek to the backyard—especially if it's cold or rainy. Separation anxiety, cognitive dysfunction, and even the food your Labrador is eating could be possible culprits as well.

Solution

If immobility is a problem, consider using more carpet between the dog's living quarters and the great outdoors to help him move more comfortably. Ramps can also be helpful. In some cases, especially with older or sick animals, the dog may just have to go more frequently, and you may have to alter your own schedule to accommodate his needs. If you suspect your dog's house soiling is a symptom of a medical condition, you should take him to the vet first to rule out anything serious.

Your puppy may soil a special bed if he is not sure where he is supposed to do his business. Supervise your pup between outings to prevent accidents.

Nuisance Barking

Remember that some barking is absolutely normal and even desirable in dogs. Dogs bark to warn us of approaching strangers and also to let us know they're happy or they need something. The problem occurs when the barking does not stop. This is what is usually meant by nuisance barking.

Labradors are not exceptionally troublesome barkers, but if they

Labs—like all dogs—bark and jump for many reasons, not the least of which is pure joy.

get into the habit, it can literally drive you and your neighbors crazy. Your Lab may nuisance bark for the following reasons:

- To express joy in living.
- To protect the yard.
- To warn you of approaching strangers.
- To tell you he's bored or lonely.
- To contact or respond to another dog.

As a rule, the more space your dog has in which to exercise, the less likely he will be to bark. The worst barkers are dogs who are kept outside on a chain. Dogs left outside at night also tend to bark; they probably find it spooky out there, and the yard is full of strange sounds that need to be responded to.

If your dog is barking because he is bored or lonely, change his environment. Play with him, take him on walks, or get him a companion. However, don't reward the barking by doing any of these things in *immediate response* to the barking. If the only time you pay attention to your dog is when he barks, you are rewarding his behavior. Even yelling out the window for him to be quiet is better than nothing so far as a dog is concerned. In fact, he may think you're joining in!

Elderly dogs suffering from canine cognitive disorder often bark for apparently no reason at all. Your older dog might also be suffering from hearing loss and may not even be aware that he is barking.

Regular bark-producing events, like the arrival of the letter carrier, can be a challenge. Whether your dog loves the letter carrier or hates him, he's anticipating the Big Event. As the magic hour approaches, he may become more and more excited. This is especially true if he's alone in the house, when this might be the highlight of the day.

Behavior Modification Solution

If your dog is barking from sheer happiness, allow him about six barks and then bring him inside. He will soon understand that overdoing the joy barking brings an unintended result. You might also try giving the joy-barker a cheese or peanut butter-filled toy. Dogs can't bark and chew at the same time, and by the time he finishes the treat, the thrill of the backyard may have worn off.

If your Lab is barking because he is bored, ignore the barking until he is quiet for a few minutes. Then bring him inside. Don't let a problem barker get the idea that continued barking brings results. Remember that any dog will begin to bark or whine if ignored long enough.

If your dog barks outside when you are away from home, keep him inside. If he barks while he's inside the house, shut the blinds to reduce the stimulation. Remember that any attention you pay to barking rewards that behavior. This doesn't mean you should never pay attention to barking. It means you should respond only to barking that is done for a legitimate purpose. Don't worry about confusing your dog. Except in the case of some elderly dogs, your dog knows why he's barking. He can easily discriminate between the kinds of barking that get rewards (attention) and those that don't. For instance, if you come out and yell at or play with a barking dog, you will encourage him to bark at you whenever he wants you to come out. The dog is then calling the shots.

Yawn to Calm

Strangely enough, yawning in the presence of nervous dogs appears to calm them down. It works with people, too. You can't yawn just once, though; you have to do it over and over before the good effect sets in.

If your dog barks at a visitor, say in a mild tone, "Good boy, no bark." Then touch him and ask him to "settle." This acknowledges that his warning has registered and that you see the danger and will deal with it appropriately. After all, it's a good thing for dogs to announce the arrival of guests. It is part of their inherited nature, after all.

Teach the "no bark" command by saying, "No bark" and rewarding your dog with a treat the instant he stops. If he continues to bark, turn your back and walk away. If possible, let him know that strangers are nearly always full of goodwill. If your letter carrier agrees, ask her to speak reassuringly to your dog or even hand him a dog biscuit. If nothing seems to work, close the blinds and barricade the dog from the room with a view. You can use a baby gate for this purpose.

Many people have had success in quieting their dogs by teaching them to "speak." Paradoxical as it may sound, the point is to teach the dog to bark appropriately. The reward is given on the command "shush." Soon, the dog will learn to associate the reward with the word "shush" and the correct response—silence. You must be consistent in teaching this behavior and always use the same commands.

Train Without Pain

Learning positive training techniques will get you better long-term results when training, and it will deepen your respect for each other. Dogs go through growth and learning stages just like people, so keep your expectations realistic.

Electronic and Medical Solutions

Never use physical punishment to stop barking. In the first place, it won't work. Punishment never teaches a dog anything except to try to avoid the punishment. Using a punishment to suppress a natural behavior will encourage a dog to resort to other, perhaps more destructive, actions to get his point across. It can make dogs neurotic or even aggressive.

For this reason (and others), I don't approve of the so-called "anti-bark" collars for most dogs. They are punishment devices. Some of them work by subjecting the dog to various levels (1 to 8 kilovolts) of "harmless" electrical shock. Although electronic anti-bark collar manufacturers use words like "stimulation," "pulse," "vibration," or even "tickle" to sell their wares, don't be fooled. These devices give your dog a jolt of juice. Even trainers who think these collars are effective caution that they shouldn't be used for long periods. They are also completely ineffective when used on a dog with separation anxiety or a neurotic condition.

Another kind of anti-bark collar contains citronella oil, which dogs hate. The collar sprays citronella mist in the general area of the dog's face when he begins to bark. Although this device is somewhat more humane than an electrical shock collar and more effective than a vibration or awful-noise collar, it's a poor second best to real training. It's also the most expensive of the anti-bark devices.

Some kinds of barking, especially those caused by separation anxiety, depression, canine cognitive dysfunction, and obsessive/compulsive disorder, respond well to drugs. (Medication does not work for "normal" barking.) Some drugs that have been used successfully include amitriptyline, clomipramine, buspirone, methylphenidate, fluoxetine, and selegiline. Each drug works on a different cause of barking. Consult with your vet to determine what, if any, medication is right for your dog.

Noise Phobia

A phobia is defined as a fearful reaction that is disproportionate to the real danger involved. Most human phobias involve things that can be dangerous but usually aren't, like spiders, snakes, close places, heights, crowds, and the like. Dogs also appear to have phobias, most of which are related to noise.

Some dogs are fearful of certain sounds. In fact, it's a rather common condition. In some cases, these noises are audible to us, and other times they are not. Dogs can be pretty choosy about exactly what loud sounds scare them. Some dog fear gunshots (for a working Labrador, gun-shyness is simply unacceptable), while others fear thunder, firecrackers, or vacuum cleaners.

Solution

Some experts suggest that dogs pick up some of their fear from their owners—if you are frightened of thunder, for example, chances are your dog will be, too. Even if you're not afraid of thunder per se, you can exacerbate your dog's fear by being overly soothing or coddling him. Such behavior only serves to convince him that something is really and truly wrong—why else would you be acting so oddly?

If you want to hunt with your Lab, test him for gun-shyness at an early age, and work to desensitize him if he seems scared of the shot.

It's much better to be upbeat and cheerful about loud noises and encourage your dog to scamper and play while the noise can be heard. This will channel his adrenalin into play behavior, which should take his mind off the impending noise disaster, whatever it is.

Studies show that herding and sporting breeds have a higher incidence of thunder phobia than the average dog, possibly because in the past they were kept outdoors during all kinds of weather. Dogs who feared thunder naturally took cover and were probably safer than their comrades who wandered around in the deluge.

Gun-shyness is something you may also have to deal with. If you plan to hunt or participate in field trials with your Labrador, start him off by associating in his mind the smell of gunpowder with great high-value treats. Get him used to smaller noises like popguns while continuing to hand out those treats. You can also associate the noise with fun and play.

The key to overcoming any kind of noise phobia is to substitute fear with play or treats. If nothing else works, you may wish to use medication. Over-the-counter substances like melatonin, for example, work well.

Training is more a matter of common sense than of elaborate theory. The simplest thing to do is to attempt to figure out why your dog is misbehaving. Your choices are then to change his behavior, your response, or the environment itself. There is always a solution!

ADVANCED TRAINING AND ACTIVITIES

for Your Labrador Retriever

L abs belong to the Sporting Group, and there's a reason for this—they are great sports! As peerless companion dogs, you have the option of participating in many different activities with your Lab, so don't stop at just one! This is a dog who can run, track, climb, jump, and dance. He can catch Frisbees and chase flyballs. He is one of the dog world's best swimmers, obedience dogs, and trackers. His horizons are broad, so don't disappoint him—get going!

THE CANINE GOOD CITIZEN® PROGRAM

The American Kennel Club's Canine Good Citizen (CGC) Program is a certification program that is designed to reward dogs who have good manners at home and in the community. The two parts of the program stress responsible pet ownership for owners and basic good manners for dogs. All dogs who pass the ten-step test may receive an official, frame-worthy certificate from the American Kennel Club.

The Canine Good Citizen test is open to all dogs, whether mixed breed or purebred, and there is no age limit, although the dog must be old enough to have received his immunizations. You will need a leash and collar (buckle or slip-type collar; no special training collars, such as a prong collar or head halter, are permitted) and a brush or comb for grooming. Your dog should be well groomed and in healthy condition.

This is a great opportunity to educate, bond with, and have fun with your dog. You'll both benefit!

DOG SHOWS (CONFORMATION)

When dog fanciers use the phrase "dog show," they are usually referring to conformation shows, which are basically beauty contests. The avowed purpose of the conformation show is to identify those dogs who most closely resemble the breed standard and who are worthy to pass along their genes to the next generation. Therefore, only non-neutered animals are allowed to compete.

Match Shows

If you and your dog are still learning, it's fun to enter a "match" rather than a show. Matches are informal affairs, and you can enter the very day of the event. They are specifically designed for novice handlers and dogs, so you can easily learn the ropes. You won't receive any "points" for winning, however, even if your dog turns out to be Best in Match.

Dog shows pop up all around the country every weekend, and they provide a great opportunity to meet people, exhibit your dog, buy great dog stuff you can't get anywhere else, and learn a lot about dogs in general. Some people handle their own dogs, while others hire a professional. However, if you are planning to handle your dog yourself, consider taking some handling classes at your local kennel club and attend a few dog shows. Handling classes can be invaluable. You'll learn dog show protocol, dress, and terminology, and you'll learn how to gait and pose your dog.

Even children can compete in events designed to display their dog-handling skills in Junior Showmanship classes.

Dr. Bernard Ziessow, the famous Labrador breeder and judge, has said that when judging a Labrador in the show ring, he looks at four aspects:

- **Conformation:** Conformation describes how well the dog "conforms" to the breed standard and whether he possesses the physical attributes necessary for him to perform his intended function. (In terms of the Labrador, this would mean hunting and retrieving game.)
- **Quality:** The way the various parts of the dog are put together.
- **Substance:** Bone structure and muscular development.

Conformation shows identify those dogs who most closely resemble the breed standard.

• **Movement:** Way of going; his gait at a trot in the show ring.

Obviously, there is some overlap here, and the various aspects described are more points of emphasis than separate features.

The first great objective of showing dogs is to have your dog win a championship. Each breed competes separately toward that goal. (Thus, your Labrador won't have to compete against a Poodle.) To do this, you enter at the "class level"—either in the Puppy, Novice, American Bred, Bred By Exhibitor, or Open class. In each class, four ribbons are awarded, but only the winner goes to the Winners' class. Because Labradors are the most popular dogs in the United States, Labrador classes are often very large. Feel proud if you get to a Winners class! Up through this point, males (dogs) and females (bitches) compete separately. All of these first-place dogs from all the previous classes compete. The winner is named the "Winners Dog" or the "Winners Bitch." These two winners are the only dogs to earn points toward a Championship.

The number of points available ranges from one to five, depending on how many Labradors are entered in all of the classes. A win of three, four, or five points at a single show is called a "major." A dog must win two majors and earn a total of 15 points to become a Champion.

The Winners Dog and Winners Bitch then compete against each other for Best of Winners, as well as against any dogs who have already earned their Championships and are entered as "specials" for the Best of Breed. The Labrador named Best of Breed is then allowed to compete against other sporting dog breeds for Best of Group. The winner of the competition faces other group winners for Best in Show.

Dogs who enter as "specials" may be competing for the informal but prestigious "national ratings" offered by various breed clubs and publications that tally up total number of points won. These are the dogs you may eventually see at Westminster.

While dogs don't have to do tricks to win at a conformation show, they need to show basic good manners. Your dog will need to become accustomed to having a stranger check him out, including teeth, and in the cases of males, testicles. Make sure your friendly Labrador leaves other dogs strictly alone—there is no sniffing and socializing allowed. It's just possible an untoward disagreement might occur.

Show and Field Champions

In England, a champion conformation dog must also have a hunting certificate. The American Kennel Club does not have any such restriction, and so the dual champions of the past have become rare in the United States.

FORMAL OBEDIENCE

The first obedience trial in the United States was held in 1933 (introduced by a Poodle breeder). Among the eight original competitors were two Labradors Retrievers. Today, obedience trials are held in conjunction with most all-breed dog shows. The American Kennel Club offers an obedience title to any purebred dog over the age of six months. Because obedience is a game where every dog can "win," it's a great sport for those who like to show their dogs off but are not keen on formal competitive events. Competitive or not, however, obedience is a highly structured activity with its own special culture. (Neutered animals *are* allowed to compete, which makes it wonderful for the average pet owner.) To become proficient in obedience, join your local kennel club and take some classes.

Obedience trials test your dog's ability to perform a prescribed set of scored exercises. In each exercise, your dog must score more than 50 percent of the possible points (ranging from 20 to 40) and obtain a total score of at least 170 out of a possible 200. Each time your dog accomplishes this, he gets a "leg" toward his obedience title. There are three legs toward winning an obedience title. In addition, there are three levels at which your dog can earn a title, each more difficult than the one before it.

Novice

At this level, your dog works to earn the Companion Dog (CD) title after his name once he has qualified at three separate obedience trials under three different judges. The Novice level is divided into six separate exercises:

- Heel on leash doing a figure 8.
- Stand for examination (without a lead).
- Heel free (Walk at heel without a lead—no figure 8 required).
- Come when called (recall) and return to heel position.
- Long sit (about 1 minute), usually done in company with a group of other dogs. The handler will be at the opposite side of the ring from the dog.
- Long down (about 3 minutes), also done in a group. The handler will be at the opposite side of the ring from the dog.

Open

At this level, your dog is working for his Companion Dog Excellent (CDX) title. In addition to his previous accomplishments

---

The Kennel Club's Good Citizen Dog Scheme

In 1992, the Kennel Club launched a new training program called the Good Citizen Dog Scheme to promote responsible dog ownership in the UK. Since then, over 52,000 dogs have passed the test, which is administered through 1,050 training organizations.

Any dog is eligible to take part in the Good Citizen Dog Scheme, a noncompetitive plan that trains owners and dogs for everyday situations and grants four awards—bronze, silver, gold, and puppy foundation assessment—based on the level of training that both dog and owner have reached together. For more information, refer to the Kennel Club's website at www.the-kennel-club.org.uk.

(which include staying for longer periods), he'll be asked to jump (both long and broad), drop down halfway back on recall, and retrieve (a snap for Labs). Earning a CDX title requires your dog to work entirely off lead. He will have to heel off lead in a figure 8 pattern, drop on recall (going "down" rather than just sitting on recall), retrieve a dumbbell from 20 feet over level ground, retrieve a dumbbell over the high jump, and jump the broad jump. He must also do longer sits (3 minutes) and downs (5 minutes) with the handler completely out of sight.

Each obedience level may be divided into "A" and "B" divisions at a trial" "A" classes are for beginners whose dogs have never received a title, while "B" classes are for more experienced handlers.

Utility

At this level, your dog is working toward a Utility Dog (UD) title. He will need to perform more difficult exercises following hand signals, as well as succeed at scent discrimination using articles made of leather and metal. Utility dogs often go on to compete and earn legs at ten shows to earn their Utility Dog Excellent (UDX) title. Dogs ranking first or second in Open B or Utility classes can earn points toward an Obedience Trial Championship (OTCH) title placed before the dog's name, which is earned by acquiring 100 points.

Your Labrador will have to be properly trained to demonstrate good manners before entering a conformation show.

Non-Regular Classes

In addition to these regular classes, there are several "fun" classes that include Brace (two dogs with one handler), Team (in which five handlers and their dogs perform the routine simultaneously), and Versatility, in which handlers are assigned six random exercises—two from Novice, two from Open, and two from Utility.

TRACKING

Tracking is formally part of obedience, but it is really a separate event. Your dog will work toward his Tracking Dog (TD) title by following a human scent laid from 30 minutes to 2 hours before the trial. The track is from 440 to 500 yards long and includes turns.

The Tracking Dog Excellent (TDX) title is earned by following an older (three to five hours) and longer (800 to 1,000 yards) track with more turns and more obstacles.

Another tracking title is the Variable Surface Tracking (VST) title, in which a dog tackles the urban jungle, walking down streets, up stairs, and other vegetation-bare areas. This track is between three and five hours old.

Because agility places stress on young, developing joints, many experts recommend waiting until your dog is 18 to 24 months old.

AGILITY

Versatility is the name of the game these days. More and more dog clubs are rewarding owners not only for encouraging their dogs to participate in what they were originally bred to do, but also to expand their horizons and compete in events like agility.

Agility has become extremely popular among dog owners. Agility has three levels: Novice, Open, and Excellent. Two types are offered at each level: standard or jumpers with weave poles. For example, at the Novice "standard" level, a dog dashes through an obstacle course consisting of ramps, seesaws, "dog-walks," tunnels, jumps, and a "pause table." The weave pole level adds the weave poles and omits the pause table, along with some other minor differences.

It's important to remember that agility places stress and compressive force on young, developing joints. Many agility experts recommend waiting until your dog is 18 to 24 months old, when his skeletal system is more mature. Begin with lower jumps and slower speeds for your young Labrador, building up only gradually. You should also check your dog daily for lameness or swelling.

In the United States, several organizations hold sanctioned agility events. These include the AKC, the United States Dog Agility Association, and the North American Dog Agility Council Inc. (NADAC).

With their powerful noses and great dispositions, Labs make excellent trackers, often taking part in search work.

FIELD TRIALS

Labrador field trials began in 1931. The general purpose of a retriever field trial is to test the merits of the dog in the job for which he was bred. Retriever field trials are thus designed to simulate as nearly as possible the conditions met in an ordinary day's shoot.

In the United Kingdom, retrievers are supposed to collect both mammals and birds, but in the United States, retrievers are used for birds only.

Retrievers should perform equally well on land and in the water, and they should be thoroughly tested on both. Dogs are expected to retrieve any type of game bird (usually pheasants or mallard ducks) under all conditions. Failure to enter rough cover, water, ice, mud, or any other unpleasant or difficult going, after having been ordered to do so several times, is sufficient cause to justify elimination. Dogs must successfully complete two "blind" retrieves, one on land and one in water, in which a dead bird is "planted" so that the dog does not know where it is, although the handler does. The dog must also complete a "mark" retrieve, in which the dog sees the bird shot or fall and then retrieves it.

The job of the Labrador is to seek and retrieve fallen game when ordered to do so. He should sit quietly on line or in the blind, walk at heel, or take up any position called for by his handler until sent to retrieve. Loud and prolonged barking or whining is sufficient cause to justify elimination. When ordered to retrieve, the Lab should retrieve quickly and briskly without overdisturbing the ground, and he should deliver the bird tenderly to the hand of the handler. He should have a soft mouth on the bird and give it willingly to the handler. At that point, he should await further orders.

Accurate marking is very important in this work. The dog should mark the fall of a bird, use the wind for scenting it, and take direction from his handler. A dog retrieving a decoy will be eliminated. (Decoys are designed to fool the ducks, not the dog.)

Most field trials are run on weekends and offer four different "stakes." Each stake is designed for a different level of experience. The most advanced ("major") stakes are the Open and Amateur Stakes. Dogs who finish in the top four places earn points toward Field Championships (handled by a professional) or Amateur Field Championships (handled by a nonprofessional, although the dog may have been professionally trained).

Each stake includes several tests. If a dog passes the first test, he's called back for the second, and so on. Most dogs are eliminated rather quickly, and by the end of the day, perhaps fewer than a dozen dogs will have successfully completed all tests. At this point, the judges award those dogs who did good work but who did not place in the top four. At any licensed or member field trial, the judges may award a "Judges' Award of Merit" in any stake to any unplaced dog for particularly excellent work.

Field Trials in the United Kingdom

The difference between American and English field trials begins with who gets selected to enter. In the United Kingdom, it's largely the luck of the draw, because registration is limited to 12 dogs per day. Many people enter over and over again and are not selected. The UK trials also approximate normal hunting conditions much more nearly than do the American-style ones, and wild animals like rabbits and hares are used, not just partridge or pheasant.

While both British and American field trial dogs share a "working Labrador" physique rather than what is commonly seen in the show ring, it is generally agreed that English field dogs are more "typey" than the American version, which according to some experts has become snipey, whippety, and "hard looking." These are largely subjective terms, but they generally refer to a dog with a racier body type, narrower muzzle, and harsher expression than is commonly seen in the show ring.

HUNTING TESTS

In 1985, the American Kennel Club instituted the retriever hunting test program. This program is the ideal venue for those who wish to participate in field trial-like events without competing at the extraordinarily tough level demanded by those tests. It is also a wonderful opportunity for novices to get some experience in the field. Instead of competing against each other as in standard field trials, the hunt test asks a dog to perform a set series of

Training for field trials can be particularly arduous, as Labs are expected to perform equally well on land and in the water.

If It's a Hunter You Want

Having your Labrador professionally trained as a gun dog takes about three to four months for a basic shooting dog course. He can begin as early as seven months of age. As the dog gets older, he can learn more advanced hand signals and whistle response.

exercises, much like in obedience trials. Any dog can enter and win if he can do the work.

Currently, hunting tests are offered at three levels: Junior Hunter (JH), Senior Hunter (SH), and Master Hunter (MH). The Junior Hunter level tests the dog on his natural retrieving abilities. He can be lightly held on a leash and then released to retrieve two single land marks and two single water marks. At the Senior Hunt level, the dog is worked without a leash. He must retrieve multiple marks from land and water and retrieve two "blind" birds. Of course, the birds aren't blind. This just means that the dog can't have seen them being "planted." At the Master level, the dog must retrieve multiple marks on land and in water and also "honor" other dogs, which basically means nothing except not taking credit for another dog's work. The dog's manners are judged quite strictly at this level.

LABRADOR CERTIFICATES

Many owners have neither the time nor the money to enter full-blown field trials, conformation competitions, or hunt tests. The Labrador Retriever Club Inc. (LRC) offers such people a certificate option.

Conformation Certificate (CC)

The conformation certificate is part of a noncompetitive conformation evaluation program open to all Labrador Retrievers, including spayed and neutered dogs. The purpose of the certificate is to promote an awareness of the desirable Labrador Retriever breed type. The certificate is awarded to any Labrador Retriever over one year of age who passes a conformation examination sanctioned by the LRC and officiated by an approved American Kennel Club judge. The dogs are judged in accordance with the breed standard. The evaluation should demonstrate that a dog possesses the basic attributes of a Labrador Retriever.

The evaluation sheet contains eight conformation and temperament categories for a judge to consider on a numerical basis. To assist in determining if a dog is worthy of receiving a CC, a judge should consider whether or not the animal possesses the basic attributes of a Labrador Retriever based on the breed standard.

The Conformation Certificate is not an official title but should be considered an accomplishment similar to the LRC Working

Certificate. It is an opportunity for owners of Labrador Retrievers who are not interested in or familiar with competitive conformation events to have their dogs evaluated and recognized as having basic Labrador Retriever conformation characteristics. Conformation Certificate examinations are designed to be held in conjunction with performance events, such as hunt tests, field trials, or agility and obedience trials. Judges are free to conduct the examination of dogs by any means they so desire; as a means of education, they may give a verbal explanation of their decision to each handler if this is requested and time permits. Judges are free to conduct examinations as formally or as informally as they like. However, dogs' names and breeding should remain unknown to the judge until after the event. Casual clothing for handlers and judges is appropriate. When an evaluation is held in conjunction with a hunt test or field trial, consideration will be given for animals who may have just performed in the field. As a result, handlers need not change clothing.

Working Certificate (WC)

The Labrador Retriever Club also offers a Working Certificate. This is an opportunity for your dog to receive recognition for the job he was bred to do (even if you don't hunt yourself). Your dog will be tested to see that he is not gun-shy, and he will be expected to retrieve a shot game bird at a distance of 50 yards or greater on land. Further, the dog will be expected to retrieve two freshly shot ducks from the water, one in immediate succession, to establish the dog's willingness to reenter water. Any reasonable command or gesture may be used to direct the dog to retrieve and return. Nothing may be thrown and no coercion may be used to encourage completion of a retrieve once the dog has been initially released to retrieve. Any dog who has satisfactorily completed both a land and water series in a field trial licensed by the American Kennel Club; who has received a placement or judge's award of merit in a field trial sanctioned by the American Kennel Club; who has successfully completed an AKC Junior Hunter Title; or who has achieved at least one leg on a Senior or Master Hunter Title shall be deemed to have satisfied the Working Certificate requirements. In addition, a Working Certificate requirement may be satisfied by establishing to the satisfaction of any current member of the Club's Board of Directors that the dog in question has performed in

Chocolates and Field Work

While chocolate Labs have a special charm all their own, the fact is that chocolates do not perform in the field as well as black or yellow Labs. As nearly all chocolates come from the same line, there may be something in that line that inhibits the ability of the dog in terms of field work. It may or may not be specifically linked to the color. Instead, it could be a genetic factor that is separate from the gene that controls color but is nonetheless passed along with it.

Kennel Club Sporting Events

The Kennel Club in the United Kingdom sponsors a variety of events for dogs and their owners to enjoy together. For complete listings, rules, and descriptions, please refer to the Kennel Club's website at www.the-kennel-club.org.uk.

Agility

Introduced in 1978 at Crufts, agility is a fun, fast-paced, and interactive sport. The event mainly consists of multiple obstacles on a timed course that a dog must handle. Different classes have varying levels of difficulty.

Flyball

Flyball is an exciting sport introduced at Crufts in 1990. Competition involves a relay race in which several teams compete against each other and the clock. Equipment includes hurdles, a flyball box, backstop board, and balls.

Obedience

Obedience competitions test owner and dog's ability to work together as a team. There are three types of obedience tests, which include the Limited Obedience Show, Open Obedience Show, and Championship Obedience Show. Competition becomes successively more difficult with each type of show.

Field Trials

Field trials are designed to test a gundog's ability to work in his natural environment and under competitive conditions. These trials are very similar to a day of hunting in the field, and a variety of game is used.

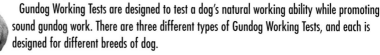

Gundog Working Tests (GWTs)

Gundog Working Tests are designed to test a dog's natural working ability while promoting sound gundog work. There are three different types of Gundog Working Tests, and each is designed for different breeds of dog.

accordance with the minimum requirements set forth above.

The Labrador Retriever Club is so interested in maintaining the working ability of the Labrador that one of its rules states, "No member of the Club shall use the title "CH" in front of the name of a registered Labrador Retriever dog until said dog, having won a conformation championship, shall also receive a working certificate or the equivalent as defined in this Article."

RALLY OBEDIENCE

On January 1, 2005, rally became a titled event in the American Kennel Club. Rally is a sport held in conjunction with obedience in which a dog and handler proceed at their own pace through a course of directional signs in a manner similar to rally car racing. These signs are numbered sequentially to show the handler where to take the dog. The dog and handler team heel from sign to sign and perform the exercises indicated on the sign at each location. Each sign contains an exercise illustrated with symbols. Your dog can earn a title in each of three levels: Novice, Advanced, and

Excellent. In addition, a dog may continue to compete in the Advanced and Excellent classes to earn a Rally Advanced Excellent title. The suffix title designations are RN, RA, RE, and RAE.

FLYBALL

Flyball is a non-AKC event that is competitive and timed. Competitors race in teams over a short course with hurdles. At the end of the run, they activate a box that releases a tennis ball, and then they return to the starting line where the next dog starts.

DANCING WITH DOGS/ MUSICAL FREESTYLE

Dog dancing aficionados say that dancing is a great way to keep your dog active, engaged, and focused. There are even dog dancing contests, seminars, and CDs available. To learn more about this sport, check with the Musical Dog Sport Association.

EXERCISE, GAMES, AND ACTIVITIES

Maybe you're not interested in organized events. That's fine, because you and your Lab can have a great time just by yourselves!

Don't forget that almost greatest of events for your Labrador: a romp on the beach.

Walking and Jogging

Walking and jogging is a great way to bond with your dog in a healthful, low-stress event that you'll both like. It has been shown that people who have a dog buddy for a walking partner do better than those people who go it alone—and your dog will enjoy it as well!

If you decide to walk or jog with your Lab, begin slowly. Work up to a half hour or so of vigorous activity several times a week.

Frisbee

Because Frisbee can be physically stressful for some dogs, play in moderation.

This popular sport can be physically stressful for canine athletes. Dogs were not meant to jump and twist, as these actions are hard on the spine. To play safely, it's important to know the physical capabilities of your dog. Young dogs in particular are at risk, so if your dog plays, don't overtax him.

Fetch

Labradors are fetching dogs in more ways than one, so it should be a snap to teach yours to fetch on command. Fetching is a natural behavior that needs little reinforcement in this breed. Having said this, I should mention that many professional trainers use a "forced retrieve" method of teaching hunting and field trial dogs. However, forced retrieve training involves pain. It can be brutal and will backfire with a more timid dog. One alternative to this "forced retrieve," which seems unnecessarily harsh, is the "play retrieve," shunned by some professionals as sloppy and unreliable.

Many dogs will chase after a toy but refuse to bring it back, preferring to play keep away. When that happens, the dog is in charge of the game, not you. To prevent this from happening, you should run in the opposite direction so that your dog will try to chase you. When he approaches, ask for the toy and praise or treat him when he does what is asked.

A newer alternative favored by many modern trainers is clicker motivational training. To use this effectively, you will have to have a large number of small, high-value treats (something better than dog biscuits) and be able to break down the desired behavior into small steps, such as taking the article from your hand, walking with it, and so on. If your dog is not clicker trained already, you'll need to introduce him to the device. (You don't actually have to use a clicker; a short sound will work as well.) To start, simply click and reward. Do this often enough so that the dog associates the sound with the treat.

Teach your puppy that games continue when he willingly brings you his prize and lets you take it from him.

Continue with the training, just remembering to break it down into bits. Training a dog for retrieve in the field is a bit different from teaching the retrieve for obedience, so you'll need to decide what your training goal is and work from there.

Tug-of-War

Some Labradors enjoy tug-of-war, but if you're training your dog to hunt and retrieve, you really want to avoid this game. Labs need to have a soft, tender mouth to give up the game, and tug-of-war teaches them to clamp down. The only time you should play tug-of-war with a retriever is if he is too soft mouthed, but Labs don't usually have that problem.

Camping

If you enjoy camping without your Lab, you'll like it even better if you can take him along. Labradors are the perfect companions for all of your outdoor adventures. In order to make your camping trip together an enjoyable experience, your Lab should be:
- Well behaved around other dogs and people.
- Not predatory when around small mammals, like squirrels.

- Healthy and up to date on vaccinations.
- In fit condition.
- Completely trustworthy off lead or kept on a leash at all times.

If your Lab meets these criteria, he's an ideal candidate for camping. All you need to do is provide for his needs, pick up after him, and restrain him on a leash when necessary.

Before You Leave

Before you leave on your trip, make sure that you have all of your Lab's paperwork, including his license, vaccination records (especially the all-important rabies tag), and contact information. Be sure your Lab is identified to the hilt—tags, microchip, or tattoos—the more the better! If you use tags, make sure they're firmly attached, because many hooks can come unattached with dismaying ease.

It's a good idea to have your vet examine your Lab before you leave. Also, if you are planning on hiking around in the back country, let appropriate people (including a park ranger) know when you expect to be back. These precautions will make the trip a fun experience for you and your dog, and they may even save your lives.

Supplies

The following items are crucial for campers:
- Extra leashes—different lengths, including a retractable lead.
- Tether—to attach to a tree or in the ground for lunch stops and so on.
- Bedding—it can be just a folded blanket or towel but should have a waterproof sheet underneath it.
- Grooming items.
- Food, treats, and water—it's best not to allow your Lab to drink from natural water sources, but you may not be able to stop him.

Many Labs excel at search and rescue work.

• First-aid kit—see Chapter 8 for more information.

If you are heading for a regular campsite, check to make sure dogs are invited. In addition, follow the posted rules, which usually require you to keep your dog on a leash. Always clean up after your dog in a campsite—other people may use it, too.

THERAPY DOGS AND SEARCH AND RESCUE DOGS

Labradors are of a size and disposition to make great therapy dogs. They are calm, gentle, and friendly. They visit hospitals, nursing homes, and even prisons! For more information on therapy dogs and to learn how to get involved, visit Therapy Dog International on the Internet at www.tdi-dog.org.

Many other Labs do very well at search and rescue work, and some even work as bomb, narcotic, and arson dogs.

As you can see, there are numerous joys to owning a Lab. These fun-loving, versatile dogs excel at a variety of endeavors, and there are virtually no limits to the kinds of sports and activities that the two of you can participate in together.

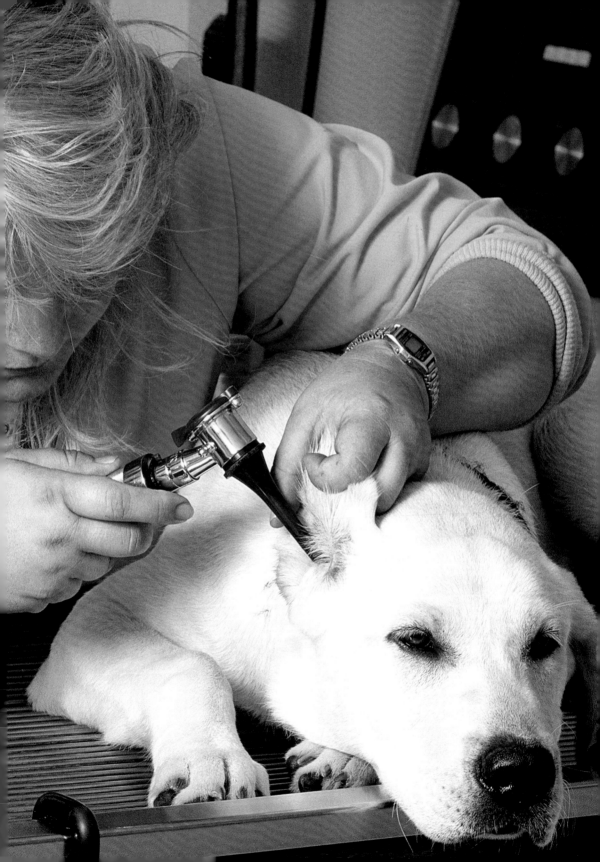

Chapter 8

HEALTH

of Your Labrador Retriever

L abradors were originally meant to be strong, healthy dogs. They had to be, as they were bred to work hard all day under tough conditions. However, as with all contemporary breeds, health problems have taken their toll. Some of the health problems seen in Labs today are genetic diseases that stem from overuse of "popular sires" and careless breeding. In other cases, the ills of modern life, like too much food—especially too much bad food—and too little exercise have resulted in obese animals prone to arthritis, diabetes, cancers, and a host of other problems.

This doesn't mean that your Lab has to be a sick dog, and most are not. What it does mean is that you should use all of your owner savvy to keep a careful eye on your dog and take him to the vet when you suspect something is wrong. You are your dog's first line of defense against illness, and your vet is your backup and support. In many cases, you can prevent your Lab from getting sick in the first place by making sure he gets a proper diet, the right amount of exercise, and appropriate preventive care, like vaccinations and anti-parasite medications.

Here is the interesting news: Labrador owners rank as the best owners in terms of their willingness to get their dogs premium medical care. Sixteen percent of Labrador Retriever owners fit into the top bracket in veterinary spending for routine veterinary care, like dental work and vaccinations, higher than any group except for Golden Retriever owners, who tied with them.

TAKING YOUR DOG TO THE VET

When deciding on a veterinary clinic for your dog, ask yourself the following questions:

- Is the staff relaxed, friendly, and compassionate?
- What services does the clinic provide?
- Are staff members specialists in orthopedics, holistic treatments, behavior, or cardiology? (It's fine if everyone is a generalist, but if this is the case, the practice

should be able to offer referrals to those specialists in time of need.)

- What are the clinic's hours? Are they open in the evenings or on weekends?
- Who answers calls when the clinic is closed?
- Does the clinic offer boarding or grooming services?
- Are telephone conferrals available?
- Does the clinic accept pet insurance?
- How close is the vet to your home?
- How many Labradors does the practice handle?

Adding up the answers to these questions may make it easier to decide on the right vet for you.

All other things being equal, choose a vet close to your home. A difference of a few minutes in travel time can mean the difference between life and death for your Labrador.

The First Visit

Annual checkups will help you maintain your Lab's health throughout his life.

Make the first visit to the vet a fun and interesting one for your dog. If all goes well, the first trip will be for a checkup only, so your dog won't have any painful associations with the visit. If you are

Neutering (Spaying and Castrating)

Unless you own a show dog, please consider spaying or castrating your Labrador. Spaying a female dog refers to the removal of the ovaries and uterus, while castrating refers to the removal of a male dog's testicles. Castrating has numerous health benefits, such as eliminating or reducing the risk of various cancers of the reproductive system, including prostate cancer in males and mammary cancer in females. It also eliminates the possibility of uterine infections in females. At one time, it was believed that dogs could not be safely neutered before the age of six months; however, modern advances in surgery have made early neutering possible.

calm and happy yourself, your mood is bound to rub off on your Labrador! It's really important to use this first visit as an opportunity to establish a cordial relationship between your vet and your dog. Your dog will have no reason to fear the vet if you don't.

Do not wait until your puppy is sick before he meets his doctor for the first time. A healthy, bouncy puppy will have no fear of the vet unless it's instilled in him by your own insecurities. Make the trip fun by giving him treats and keeping your tone of voice excited and happy when speaking to him.

During that all-important first visit, your vet will weigh your puppy and take his temperature and pulse. She will listen to the heart and lungs through a stethoscope and palpate the organs to feel for any abnormalities. Your vet will also check your dog's genitals to make sure there is no unusual discharge, and in the case of unneutered males, she will ensure that the testicles are properly descending. In addition, she will examine your dog's eyes and ears and check the skin for parasites and general tone. The dental check is critical, too. Baby teeth sometimes don't fall out when they should, and older dogs may need their teeth cleaned.

VACCINATIONS

Vaccinations save lives. Before the days of effective veterinary vaccines, dogs were victims of canine distemper, hepatitis, and rabies. Now these diseases are rare. When parvo first emerged on the scene in the late 1970s, many dogs died before a vaccine was developed. While there is an ongoing discussion about how often and against what diseases your dog needs to be vaccinated, you owe it to your dog and your community to do your research and make an informed choice. Of course, as with any medical procedure, adverse reactions or side effects can occur. Usually these are minor, especially when compared with the risks of developing the disease. Consult with your veterinarian to inquire about his vaccine protocol, and don't be afraid to ask questions!

Vaccination Protocol

While vaccination scheduling is a matter of controversy(and is constantly changing), here are the current recommendations for most dogs.

Puppies 4 to 20 Weeks of Age

The vaccination series begins between six and eight weeks of age. Typically, the last vaccination is given between 14 and 16 weeks of age. These early vaccines should protect against canine distemper virus, canine adenovirus, parainfluenza, and canine parvovirus. In cases where your dog is exposed to others in a closed area, a vaccine against bordetella is recommended. The rabies vaccine should be given in accordance with individual state laws, usually between 16 and 26 weeks of age. Newer vaccines that are effective against specific forms of leptospirosis are given in certain affected areas. Check with your vet.

Check with your veterinarian to learn your Lab's vaccination options.

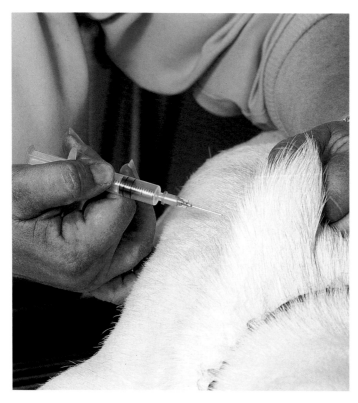

Dogs 20 Weeks to 2 Years of Age

Young adults need booster shots to ensure lifelong immunity against the same diseases they were vaccinated against as puppies.

Dogs Over 2 Years of Age

If your dog has had his puppy shots and boosters, you and your vet may wish to forgo further vaccination for three or four years. It is increasingly recognized that annual vaccinations are not necessary, although annual checkups certainly are!

Diseases to Protect Against

Although vaccination protocols differ from place to place and even from vet to vet, consider vaccinating your Labrador puppy against the following diseases.

Rabies

Although rabies is not common, it's always fatal. It is transmitted through saliva into the blood stream, usually by a bite. Rabies affects the central nervous system with lethal precision. Once symptoms appear, it's always fatal—in dogs and in people. All mammals are susceptible to rabies, although some (like foxes and raccoons) are more likely to get it than others (like squirrels and groundhogs).

It is the law in most parts of the United States to give your dog a rabies shot. He should receive his first rabies vaccination at about four months of age. Rabies shots must be renewed periodically, but how often depends upon the type of vaccination and the law in your jurisdiction. Some states require yearly boosters, while other states mandate them only every three years.

Your "great outdoorsman" is susceptible to the pests and predators that share his territory. Be sure he's appropriately protected with the necessary vaccines.

Hepatitis

Puppies are particularly at risk for hepatitis, a highly contagious viral disease that is shed though the stool, saliva, and urine. It does not affect people. Hepatitis causes injury to the liver, kidneys, and lining of the blood vessels. In some cases, the disease is rather mild, while other times it can be fatal.

Hepatitis presents a wide range of signs, some of which are similar to those of canine distemper. They include lethargy, bloody diarrhea, high fever, and lack of appetite. The affected animal will move with pain and may present a "tucked-up" belly caused by swelling of the liver. The dog may also squint. As with most viral diseases, supportive treatment like IV fluids is all that can usually be given.

Distemper

Canine distemper is actually related to the human measles virus. It is the leading killer of dogs worldwide. Distemper affects nearly all of the body tissues, and once a dog is affected, he may never be the same, especially if the virus reaches the brain tissues. Signs of distemper include fever, lack of appetite, watery discharge from the eyes and nose, coughing, vomiting, diarrhea, and lethargy. Later stages include seizures and paralysis, followed by death. Both the nose pad and paw pads harden, accounting for the original name of the disease: hardpad. Again, supportive treatment like IV fluids is all that can usually be given.

Parvovirus

This contagious disease attacks rapidly reproducing cells, such as those lining the intestinal tract, bone marrow, and lymph nodes. It is transmitted through contaminated feces and droplets that can be carried on the dog's hair and feet. The disease is most dangerous to puppies under the age of five months. Signs include severe depression, pain, vomiting, tucked-up abdomen, high fever, and profuse diarrhea.

Replacing fluids lost through diarrhea and vomiting is probably the single most important treatment. Intravenous administration of a balanced electrolyte solution is preferred. Your vet may also use antibiotic therapy to help control secondary bacterial infections. If vomiting is severe, your vet can give drugs to slow the vomiting. However, even with the best professional care, a large percentage of parvo-infected dogs will die.

It should be noted that even with the best vaccination protocol, all puppies will have a window of susceptibility of several days where they will be vulnerable to the disease. Using the newer high titer vaccines may shorten the window of susceptibility in many puppies.

Coronavirus

This disease bears a superficial resemblance to parvovirus, but it is not nearly as serious. It is usually spread when a puppy samples infected feces. Coronavirus is generally self-limiting, meaning that i[...] [wi]thout serious damage in most cases, and vac[...] [rar]ely uncommon and usually unnecessary. [...] [treatme]nt for this disease—only supportive c[...]

Leptospi[...]

Leptos[...] [inf]ection that can damage the kidneys, [...] [thoug]h it is not usually fatal. Infection occurs w[...] [come]s from the urine of an infected host through [...] [Dog]s typically contract leptospirosis through direct co[ntact with th]e urine of infected animals, but not all dogs who encounter it will be become sick. Instead, they may turn into carriers, shedding the virus in their urine and infecting other animals in turn.

Some of the more common signs of leptospirosis include fever, weight loss, dehydration, vomiting, diarrhea, and abdominal pain. However, it is possible for an infection to exist in a dog who has no clinical signs. In its most dangerous form, leptospirosis can shut down the kidneys. Treatment includes antibiotics, and in cases of kidney failure, dialysis. A vaccine is available for some forms of leptospirosis; however, many vets do not recommend its use, especially for young puppies. However, if your dog is apt to encounter wildlife such as voles, raccoons, skunks, and opossums, you should consider getting your dog vaccinated against the *grippotyphosa* strain of leptospirosis.

The best "cure" for leptospirosis is prevention by protecting your dog with a vaccine.

Bordetellosis (Kennel Cough)

This disease is commonly known as kennel cough because of its extremely contagious nature. It affects the upper respiratory system, and while it is not too serious in older dogs (it's like a bad cold), it can be very detrimental to puppies. Most grooming shops and boarding kennels want to see proof of vaccination before they will take your dog.

The most obvious sign of kennel cough is a horrible deep, hacking cough. Treatment may include antibiotics for the bacterial component of the disease. Some vets tell their clients to give the dog 1 tablespoon of cough suppressant to calm down the coughing.

Kennel cough can be caused by a bacterial organism

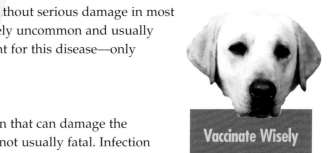

Vaccinate Wisely

A debate is currently ongoing as to what is the safest vaccination protocol. Talk to your veterinarian about what you can do for your Lab, taking into consideration the advice in this book. Your veterinarian can keep you on track with what's necessary for your Lab.

(bordetella), or it can be caused by either the canine adenovirus (hepatitis virus) or the parainfluenza virus.

Lyme Disease (Borrelia)

This disease, while observed everywhere in the United States, is most prevalent in the mid-Atlantic region. Symptoms include arthritis-like pain and swelling, fever, and loss of appetite. Vaccination may be recommended for dogs who spend a lot of time in the woods. Lyme disease is treated with doxycycline, an antibiotic.

PARASITES

Parasites cause problems that can result in something as simple as mild itching or something much more severe, such as death. External parasites include mites (sarcoptic, demodex, ear, or cheyletiella), fleas, and ticks. Internal parasites usually include worms like roundworm, hookworm, whipworm, and heartworm. Many of these parasites can be prevented or kept under control with preventive medications.

External Parasites

Inspect your Lab for fleas and ticks after he's been outdoors.

External parasites live on but not inside your dog's body. With the exception of some species of mites, they are usually visible.

Fleas

Over 2,200 species of flea exist worldwide, but fortunately, most of them live elsewhere than on your dog. In fact, there is no reason for the contemporary dog to become afflicted with fleas. It still happens, though, and the ingestion of even one flea containing a tapeworm larva is enough to transmit tapeworm. It can even cause an allergic dog to develop itchy flea dermatitis, which is caused by certain enzymes in flea saliva.

The most common flea to attack dogs is the cat flea (*Ctenocephalides felis*). The cat flea can lay 50 eggs a day for 100 days. These smooth, tiny eggs usually fall onto the carpet or into the couch. A few days later, they hatch into larvae. The larvae live largely on flea feces. About a week later, the larvae spin themselves tiny cocoons and snooze away for a variable period of time, usually a couple of weeks but occasionally several months. When they wake up, they're hungry, and your dog is on the menu!

One of the most important things to remember when dealing with fleas is this: Don't wait for your pet to start scratching! Even if you use a good flea preventive, it doesn't hurt to check your dog for fleas every time you groom him. Glide your thumbs against the growth pattern of the fur, or use a flea comb. The groin, base of the tail, and neck are popular flea hangouts. Even if you don't see any actual fleas, the black deposits they leave will provide a clue to their presence.

In the old days, people tried to control fleas with topical sprays, powders, dips, collars, and yard sprays. While some people still resort to these old-fashioned methods, most up-to-date owners choose to control fleas with a capsule, or they use a spot-on liquid applied to the skin between the shoulder blades. Some products are available from your veterinarian, although you can get others (although they are somewhat shorter lived and less effective) at the pet supply or grocery store. Some people have also had luck with natural alternatives to conventional flea or tick medications. Garlic, for example, has been popular for centuries. Not all natural alternatives are equally effective, however. It's important to consult with your veterinarian before selecting a particular remedy.

Ticks

Ticks carry Lyme disease, Rocky Mountain spotted fever, ehrlichiosis, haemobartonellosis, babesiosis, tick paralysis,

A Flee-Free Zone

One great reason to live in Denver is that it is almost flea free. Fleas can't stand the high altitude!

hepatozoonosis, and a host of other diseases. They don't annoy a dog on the surface as much as fleas do, because they don't scamper around or deposit feces everywhere. However, this is why they're easy for humans to overlook.

Ticks have four life stages:

- Egg
- Six-legged larva
- Eight-legged nymph
- Adult

Dogs most frequently meet up with ticks when they wander into woodlands and brush. Ticks have a special sensory device (called "Haller's organ") that allows them to sense humidity, odors, heat, movement, and presence of a host. Ticks climb up to the tips of grass or the edge of a twig and wait for an animal or human victim to pass by. At that point, they drop off the twig or blade of grass and attach themselves, burrowing close to the skin. Then, they actually insert their heads beneath the skin to gorge on blood.

If a tick attacks your Labrador, pull it off with a pair of fine-tipped tweezers. Wear gloves if possible. Don't bother trying to smother the tick with petroleum jelly or burning it. Grip it as close to the head as possible. (You want to avoid crushing the tick and forcing its bacteria-laden contents into your Labrador.) Once the tick is out, throw it in some alcohol to kill it, or flush it down the toilet. While ticks may not die if flushed down the toilet, they're not going anywhere, either. Clean the area of the bite with a disinfectant and wash your own hands. The bite wound may develop into a welt from the tick's saliva, but this doesn't mean the tick's head is stuck in there. Give it some time; it should heal in about a week. If you believe that an infection or abscess is forming, however, take your dog to the vet.

Lice

Lice are not particularly common in dogs, but if your Lab does become infested, intense itching and irritation may occur. These chewing creatures spends their entire life cycles on the dog—from the egg stage to the adult stage—and live for about a month. As the dog scratches, he can open the way to bacterial, viral, or fungal infections.

Lice can be discouraged with ordinary flea products. By

the way, the human head louse or crab louse can also infect a dog if it can't find anything better.

Mites

These arachnids appear in various species, several of which are troublesome to dogs.

- **Demodex canis (mange mite):** Mange mites are nearly always present somewhere on a dog (you have them, too—in your eyelashes and on your eyebrows), but they don't usually cause trouble, since the immune system keeps them well under control. Sometimes, however, the immune system doesn't do its job well. In that case, the mites multiply and crowd the hair follicles, causing them to fall out. The result is hair loss and itchy, swollen, red skin.

  A localized form of mange may appear on puppies who have an immature immune system, but it will probably resolve itself without treatment. A more serious, generalized form usually shows up on older dogs who also have a compromised immune system. This form requires intensive therapy involving dips in mite and tick killer. A complete cure may take up to six months. Generalized demodex is often a sign that the dog has another problem, like an autoimmune condition or a serious underlying disease, like cancer.

A healthy skin and coat are no accident—they're the direct result of proper nutrition and exercise, as well as careful grooming.

- **Sarcoptes scabiei (sarcoptic mange):** Sarcoptic mange is caused by the scabies mite, also known as the "itch mite." Both humans and dogs can get sarcoptic mange. People can contract a temporary case from their pets that lasts about six days, although these mites do not actually reproduce on humans. Puppies and young children are more likely to be affected than adults of either species.

  In dogs who are affected by the scabies mite, the female burrows into the skin and lays her eggs. When they hatch into larvae, the larvae dig around and form nasty lesions, causing secondary infections. Affected dogs develop matted hair

and a yellowish crust on their skin. This mange is treated with special shampoos, pills, or injections. A good insecticide needs to be applied to the entire area (including bedding) where the dog lives to prevent reinfection.

- *Cheyletiella yasguri* **(walking dandruff):** This mite's charming name is indicative of its uncharming habit of producing crud and hair loss on your dog. Fortunately, it doesn't cause the severe itchiness of the other mites and doesn't cause any really serious health problems. Your vet can easily treat it with a special pesticide.

- *Otodectes cynotis* **(ear mites):** The ear mite infests both the external ear and the ear canal, nibbling away at the loose skin there. Dogs with ear mites shake their heads and dig at their ears. There will be a nasty discharge or even a hematoma or swelling in the ear from self-mutilation.

To treat ear mites, the ear needs to be thoroughly cleaned and then treated with a good commercial ear mite killer. Over-the-counter treatments are available. However, because there are many causes of itchy ears that require different treatment protocols (and because home treatment can complicate the diagnosis for the vet), dogs with ear problems should be examined by a vet prior to treatment.

Internal Parasites

Parasites are so clever that they hide inside your dog where you can't see them. Just because you can't see them doesn't mean they can't do any harm, though. The danger with parasites is that they can do quite a lot of damage before you notice they are even present at all. This is an important reason to keep your dog on parasite preventive all year round.

Tapeworm (Dipylidium caninum)

Dogs can acquire tapeworms from eating infected fleas (or more rarely, lice). A tapeworm infestation doesn't have many signs, and you probably won't even know your pet is affected unless you notice the rice-like segments of the worms in your dog's feces or near his anus. Your vet can prescribe a special dewormer to rid your dog of them.

Another common species, *Taenia pisiformis,* can be picked up by ingesting infected rabbits and rodents.

Roundworm (Toxocara canis)

Roundworms, or ascarids, are the most common internal parasites. They're usually harmless in adult dogs but can be dangerous when they are passed to puppies through their mothers. Nearly all puppies are born with roundworms, and severely affected puppies can die from them. Labradors as young as two weeks can start deworming treatment, which is continued every couple of weeks until the eggs are no longer found in the stool sample. Infected puppies typically have a rough coat, bad breath, diarrhea, vomiting, and a potbelly. They are usually infected through the placenta before birth and from the mother's milk afterward. (This is true even if the mother has been de-wormed.

Several commercial preparations are available to treat roundworms.

Whipworm (Trichuris vulpis)

Whipworms, which can be found all over North America, live in the large intestine and cecum (a pouch at the beginning of the large intestine). The whipworms, which grow to 3 inches long, actually stab through the intestine, feeding on blood and fluids. A severe infection can cause anemia, pain, and weight loss. Some dogs will also develop periodic, smelly diarrhea.

Whipworms do not attack humans, but that's the only good thing I can say about them. They are hard to get rid of, too. Each female whipworm may produce eggs that are shed in the dog's stool. These eggs may survive in the soil for up to five years waiting to infect a passing dog. There is no effective method for killing whipworm eggs in the soil. The eggs are resistant to most cleaning methods, and reinfection is likely. To prevent exposure, any feces in the yard should be picked up on a daily basis. Consult with your veterinarian for treatment and control of whipworm.

Hookworm (Ancylostoma caninum)

Hookworms get their name from the hook-like "teeth" they use to attach to the intestinal wall. Hookworms are found mostly in warmer climates. They are very small (usually about 1/8 of an inch), but they can extract enormous amounts of blood from your

Working Labs are exposed to many more sources of potential parasites, and so they must be carefully monitored for infection.

Adult hookworms do not infect humans; however, the larvae can burrow into human skin. This causes itching, commonly called ground itch, but the worms do not mature into adults.

dog, causing intestinal distress, bloody diarrhea, and in severe cases, anemia. Dogs can become infected with hookworm orally, through the skin, through the mother dog's placenta, and through the mother's milk. It has been reported that one adult female hookworm can produce as many as 20,000 eggs a day!

Your vet can detect hookworms easily though a microscopic examination of a stool sample. Adults can be killed with several medications given orally or injected. Usually, the dog will require another treatment within two to four weeks. Most heartworm prevention products contain a drug that will prevent hookworm infections. However, these products will not kill adult hookworms, so dogs must be treated for adult hookworms first. The environment may also be treated, and some are even safe to use on grass.

Heartworm (Dilofilaria immitis)

Heartworm disease is caused by the parasite *Dirofilaria immitis,* which is transmitted from dog to dog by mosquitoes. When a mosquito draws blood from an infested dog, it also sucks up some small, immature worms called microfilariae, which develop into larvae once inside the mosquito. When the mosquito attacks a new dog, the larvae are injected. It takes six to seven months for the larvae to mature. Eventually, the heartworms take up residence in the right side of the heart and the adjacent blood vessels and pulmonary arteries, where they cause cardiovascular weakness, compromised lung capacity, and eventual organ failure and death.

Signs of heartworm include chronic cough, exercise intolerance, and collapse. While many dogs show few signs until the disease is well advanced, the infected animal is still harboring the dangerous worms and allowing other dogs to become infected. Treatment for heartworm is expensive and risky. Prevention, on the other hand, is easy—you can use one of several monthly oral or topical treatments available from your vet.

Ringworm (Microsporum canis)

Despite the name, ringworm is a fungal infection usually characterized by circular hair loss and scaly skin. It is not usually itchy. Most cases disappear by themselves but more severe cases can be treated with anti-fungal medications. If your dog gets ringworm, have him (and all the other dogs and cats in your home) treated, and then clean your house thoroughly. This includes getting the air filters changed and disinfecting animal bedding, brushes, and combs with bleach. Ringworm spores can float around in the air for years.

Giardia (Giardia lamblia)

Giardia is a common protozoan parasite that can infect any mammal, including humans. (In fact, it is possible for dog owners to contract it from their pets.) Giardia has two life stages: the cyst and the trophozoite. Dogs can become infected if they drink cyst-contaminated water, lick cyst-contaminated feces, or devour cyst-infected prey. When the giardia enter the dog's gastrointestinal system, they enter a new phase of life and reproduce rapidly.

The main signs of giardiasis are vomiting and diarrhea. Infected humans report cramping and nausea also, but these symptoms are difficult to detect in dogs. If the condition is not treated, infected animals can suffer weight loss and continued periods of vomiting and diarrhea. A stool sample is sometimes used for diagnosis, although even that can be hit or miss. The ELISA blood test is more accurate, because it looks for a specific protein particular to giardia. This test is quite a bit more expensive than the fecal test, however. Several drugs are available to treat giardiasis, and there is also a vaccine available. Discuss these options with your vet.

To protect your pet from contracting giardiasis in the first place, keep your yard picked up and prevent your dog from drinking contaminated water sources. This is tougher than it sounds; even pristine mountain streams and tap water can contain the organism.

Zoonotic Diseases

Some diseases, such as ringworm, can affect both humans and dogs and can be passed from one species to another. These are called zoonotic diseases. Children are most at risk, because they tend to have very close contact with dogs and aren't always as hygienic as they might be. To reduce the chances of cross-contamination, be sure to keep children's play areas separate from places where the dog is allowed to eliminate, as most zoonotic diseases are passed through contact with feces.

COMMON DISORDERS AND DISEASES

There are literally thousands of diseases that affect canines, and over 400 of them are genetic. As Labradors are the most popular breed in America, they are also prone to getting many of them. That does not mean that your Lab is actually going to contract all or even most of them, and he might not get any! The following are some of the most common diseases affecting Labradors.

Allergies

Like human beings, dogs can become allergic to things in their environment. And Labradors, especially female Labradors, tend to be more susceptible to allergies than many other breeds.

Allergic dogs exhibit intense itching and hair loss, and while allergies can't be cured, they can be managed. The most effective treatment involves removing the allergen from the dog's environment (which is not always possible) or submitting the dog to a series of hyposensitization shots. This is effective about 60 percent of the time. Another approach is the use of antihistamines or alternate-day glucocorticoid therapy. There is even a test available that can determine in five minutes if your dog has allergies. The test is not expensive, and it can be valuable in helping your vet determine what is ailing your dog.

The following are some of the most common allergies affecting dogs.

Atopic Dermatitis

Constant scratching is a clear indication that your dog is suffering from a skin problem.

Atopic dermatitis (AD) is a very common skin condition in dogs caused by airborne allergens like dust mites, mold, or pollen. While some dogs seem to be able to tolerate a lot of that stuff, others can't—just like people. The first clinical signs of AD appear when the dog is between six months and three years of age.

In the beginning, you will likely notice that your dog seems to be itchy; he may rub his face or lick his feet. Then, you may observe some red-looking spots on different areas of your dog's body as a result of a reaction to the allergen. Reddened, irritated skin and skin lesions occur due to scratching at and chewing on those itchy areas. AD is often worse during the summer, when pollen and mold levels increase.

The preferred method of handling this and any allergy is to remove the allergen from the dog. With fleas, this is comparatively easy—with pollen, it isn't. In some cases, your dog can receive a series of shots to help build up resistance, but it's not a guarantee.

Contact Allergy

In this kind of allergy, the dog reacts to an irritant that actually touches the skin. It is not as common as AD.

Flea Allergy

This is one of the most common canine allergies. Some dogs start itching madly after one flea bite. The obvious way to handle it is to make sure your dog doesn't get fleas.

Food Allergy

Your Labrador may suffer from food allergies. (If the allergy is seasonal, it's not a food allergy.) In addition to the typical redness and itching characteristic of most canine allergic reactions, a food-allergic dog may also experience vomiting or diarrhea. In order to trace the offending ingredient, you need to conduct a food trial for at least eight weeks, giving nothing (including treats) except the recommended diet—usually a novel form of protein (like herring or emu) and a bland carbohydrate, like rice. Alternatively, you could try eliminating beef, wheat, and corn from your allergic dog's diet, because these are common allergens. Remember to checks treats for these forbidden ingredients.

Omega-3s for Itching

A recent study by veterinary researchers at Colorado State University showed that dogs who were supplemented with omega-3 fatty acids received relief from itching.

Hot Spots

These frightening-looking skin sores are usually caused by irritation, allergies, or dirt in the skin. The dog will scratch himself and make the condition worse by infecting the sores. If hot spots appear, wash them thoroughly with shampoo, rinse, and dry them. You may want to use a drying powder you can obtain from your vet.

Pyoderma

Pyoderma is a staph infection of the skin, and it is the most common skin problem affecting dogs. It causes small pustules or lesions that can develop into scabs and crusts. Pyoderma usually (but not always) produces itching and is often a symptom of a deeper problem, such as an allergy. To treat pyoderma itself, a course of oral antibiotics and frequent antibacterial shampoos over a period of three weeks are usually prescribed by a veterinarian.

Cancer

Cancer is the number-one killer of dogs ten years of age and older. In fact, dogs are three times more likely to get cancer than people are! Labradors seem especially susceptible to mast cells, nasal cavity tumors, lymphoma, and oral fibrosarcoma. Other tumors (cancerous and otherwise) reported in Labs include canine cutaneous histicytoma, lipoma, squamous cell carcinoma of the digit, thymoma, limbal melanoma, adrenal tumor, and insulinoma.

According to the Veterinary Cancer Society, here are common signs of cancer in small animals (and notice how similar these signs are to cancer in human beings):

- Abnormal swellings that persist or continue to grow
- Bleeding or discharge from any bodily opening
- Difficulty breathing, urinating, or defecating
- Difficulty eating or swallowing
- Loss of appetite
- Offensive odor from the mouth
- Persistent lameness or stiffness
- Reluctance to exercise or loss of stamina
- Sores that don't heal
- Weight loss

If you observe any of these signs in your Lab, contact your veterinarian. Cancer is not necessarily a death sentence, especially if proper treatment is administered, which may include surgery, radiation, and chemotherapy.

Keep a close eye on all generations of the Labs in your family.

Skin Cancer

Skin cancer is a broad term that covers any tumors of the skin and its associated structures (glands, hair follicles, and connective tissue). This is the most common kind of cancer in dogs. Most victims are over the age of six, although certain types occur in younger animals, too.

The cause for most types of cancer is unknown, although exposure to sunlight plays a role in two types (squamous cell carcinoma and hemangioma). Light-skinned dogs like yellow Labs are more vulnerable, although all three types of Labs have thick fur that helps protect them. You can't diagnose skin cancer yourself from harmless lumps and benign tumors, so report any suspicious lumps to your veterinarian for a thorough checkup. This may include a fine needle aspirate to examine cells, a complete blood count, serum chemistry panel, urinalysis, and chest x-rays (to see if the tumor has spread to the lungs). Treatment for skin cancer will vary depending its type and stage. It may include surgery, radiation therapy, chemotherapy, cryosurgery (freezing), and photodynamic therapy.

Cardiovascular Disease

No one can survive long without a healthy heart, including Labrador Retrievers. Of the many kinds of cardiovascular disease Labs can get, the most common are tricuspid dysplasia, a congenital condition usually affecting males, pericardial effusion, pulmonic stenosis, and a particular condition peculiar to Labs called bypass tract macro reentrant tachycardia, a problem of abnormal conduction of electricity leading to dysrhythmia.

A Healthy Heart

A healthy dog has a healthy heart. Find out from your Lab's breeder if any heart problems run in his family, and be sure to share this information with your veterinarian, who can monitor your dog for signs of a problem.

Heart Failure

The heart is basically a pump, and when it is unable to pump adequate amounts of blood to the tissue, heart failure occurs. Millions of dogs of every age and breed are affected every year. Heart failure leads to the retention of fluid in the lungs, chest cavity, or abdominal cavity.

Heart failure can be caused by a variety of different things. Some dogs are born with defective hearts, while in others, the heart valves degenerate, the lining around the heart gives out, or the heart muscle weakens. Heartworm disease is also a major factor. In certain cases, heart failure is caused by arrhythmia, a condition in which the electrical rhythms of the heart are disturbed. Signs of heart failure include fatigue, coughing, loss of appetite, swelling of the abdomen, and shortness of breath. Many dogs also lose weight. Your vet can confirm a diagnosis through the use of x-rays, blood pressure measurement, electrocardiogram, or an ultrasound examination to examine the heart and lungs.

Heart failure is treated with diuretics, nitroglycerine (in a paste form), and certain drugs that block some of the harmful hormones circulating in the heart. Certain dietary supplements, such as the following, may also be helpful (but consult your veterinarian first):

- **Coenzyme Q10:** This is a natural substance that may help the heart muscle use energy.
- **Fish oil:** Fish oil helps prevent muscle wasting by reducing levels of TNF (tumor necrosis factor).
- **L-Carnitine:** This is a substance critical to the mitochondria

161

Low-Salt Diets

If you decide to feed your dog a low-salt diet, include foods like potatoes, rice, pasta, cottage cheese, and vegetables. Most dogs with heart failure tend to lose weight over time, because the disease actually increases the dog's metabolism. (This condition is called cardiac cachexia). As a result, you need to encourage your dog to eat. Because low-sodium diets are not very palatable (to any of us), you can add some chicken fat in small amounts to improve the taste of his food. The fat also increases the number of calories in the food, so the dog will have to eat proportionately less to maintain his weight.

Dogs with heart disease usually have a lower exercise tolerance and need to take it a little easier. Make sure your Lab does not overexert himself, and provide him with plenty of water at all times.

transport of fatty acids, important energy sources for the heart muscle. (Avoid D-Carnitine or DL-Carnitine; these forms can be dangerous.)

- **Taurine:** Taurine is very helpful in patients with documented low levels of this important amino acid. Taurine regulates the heartbeat and helps take in calcium when oxygen levels are reduced, thus protecting the heart from calcium overload.

It's also important to drastically reduce the amount of salt a congestive heart failure dog ingests. Most commercial foods, especially canned foods, contain about ten times the amount of salt an adult dog needs. Talk to your vet about a special diet for your dog.

Cold Water Tail (Limber Tail Syndrome, Dead Tail, Broken Tail)

This relatively common ailment occurs in many sporting dog breeds (at least in the ones with tails). Labs with this condition have tails that either hang limply from the base or stand out horizontally for 3 or 4 inches and then drop as if broken. It can appear after the dog has been swimming or bathed or even after a day's hard work that involves a whole lot of wagging. No one really understands the cause of this ailment, but it seems to have something to do with the tail muscle. The condition is painful, but most dogs return to normal within a few days. This is a condition that is unfamiliar to many vets, who may misdiagnose it as a fracture or even a spinal cord injury, but the real problem appears to be in the muscle. Anti-inflammatory drugs prescribed by your vet may ease the pain and shorten recovery time.

Dental Disease

Dental disease is the most common problem veterinarians treat. Discolored teeth, foul breath, and red, inflamed gums are dead giveaways that some sort of dental disease is present. What may not be obvious is that all of these conditions are due to an accumulation of bacteria in the mouth. Bacteria live on food, and what's a better source of bacteria food than the warm, dark, food particle-enriched canine mouth?

Immediately after your dog eats, plaque begins to form. With the addition of calcium salts from saliva and bacteria, plague turns into hard tartar. As the bacteria chew into the tiny crevices between the teeth and gumline, a painful inflammation of the gums may occur called gingivitis. The main symptom is bleeding.

Periodontitis

If gingivitis is not treated, it may develop into periodontitis. This is a severe, painful, and irreversible condition that can affect your dog's heart, kidneys, and liver. Many dogs even become aggressive due to the pain they're suffering. You can prevent periodontitis by brushing your dog's teeth daily, but if you ignore your dog's dental hygiene and it sets in, only a veterinarian can halt its progress. This is why the best time to start a dental program is when your dog is a puppy. The next best time is right now, so it's important to brush your dog's teeth regularly. In addition, provide your Lab with toys and treats that aid in the prevention of periodontal disease, like strong Nylabones or Quest Edibles. Never give your dog anything harder to chew than his own tooth enamel, though. That includes most "sterilized bones." They can cause tooth breakage.

Cold water tail syndrome is a common ailment in sporting breeds that can occur after a dog has been swimming.

Infections of the Carnassial Tooth

The carnassial tooth is the biggest tooth in your dog's mouth; it has three roots, one of which extends up into the bone of the skull right in front of the eye. It's also called the fourth premolar, and dogs use it to break up large pieces of meat or bone. This tooth, or more properly, its root, is extremely vulnerable to infection and abscesses, which usually take place below the gumline where you can't see anything. You will, however, notice the swelling just below the eye. People unfamiliar with the carnassial abscess often think it is an eye infection or puncture wound. In some cases, the abscess will even open a hole in the skin from which you can see fluid draining. Untreated, a carnassial abscess can be very dangerous, possibly blinding your dog or worse.

The most likely victim of a carnassial tooth abscess is an older dog who has not received regular dental care. The usual option is to pull the entire tooth, which is quite a difficult procedure. It's hard to remove because it usually has to be broken in half first, and if every bit isn't taken out, the problems will continue. Some owners opt for a root canal, which will save the tooth, but this procedure can be expensive. Both therapies must be followed by antibiotics.

Regular dental examinations performed by a vet will help keep your Lab's teeth healthy.

Ear Infections

Ear infections occur when moisture in the ears allows bacteria and yeast to build up. With their floppy ears and love of water, Labradors are more likely to get such infections than say, a Pharaoh Hound. Signs of ear infection include head shaking, scratching, and upon close examination, a foul or yeasty odor emanating from the ear.

Some Labs seem especially prone to ear infections. The first step in preventing ear infections, then, is to keep the ears clean and dry. Check your Lab's ears frequently, and remove excess debris with cotton balls. Don't dig around inside the ear, though. It won't do any good, because the canine ear canal is shaped like the letter L and you could consequently injure delicate tissues. While you're cleaning, don't be afraid to actually smell the ear. A foul odor that resembles rotten fruit indicates trouble. Keep the ear dry with a non-alcohol commercial preparation.

If routine cleaning doesn't keep your Lab's ears healthy, take him to the vet.

Labs who spend a lot of time in the water are more susceptible to ear infections. Use a drying agent in the ear after swimming.

Endocrine System Disorders

The endocrine system produces the hormones that keep the body running right. When this system goes awry, the results can be devastating.

Diabetes Mellitus

One in every 200 dogs develops diabetes, and most are between the ages of seven and nine at the time of diagnosis. (Most dogs have Type 1 diabetes.) The cause is unknown, but obese dogs and females are at greater risk. Labs are especially at high risk of developing this disease, with old, unspayed females most at susceptible.

If your Lab has diabetes, it means that there is a deficiency of insulin or an insensitivity to insulin. Insulin is a hormone produced in the islet cells of the pancreas. Both too much or too little of this critical substance is lethal. Insulin controls blood concentrations of glucose (blood sugar), the main fuel for the body. All food breaks

Pet Health Insurance

If you haven't noticed already, vet care can get pretty pricey, not because the vets are making fortunes, but because we have new high-tech treatments that were once reserved only for humans. These treatments include radiation therapy, hip replacements, and kidney transplants. Although currently only about 3 percent of pet owners have health insurance for their animals, it may be a good idea. Pet insurance companies work pretty much like human ones, charging premiums, deductibles, exclusions, and different levels of coverage. Check with your vet to determine whether or not this might be a good option for you.

down into sugar and travels to cells to provide energy. Insulin controls the amount of glucose by preventing overproduction by the liver. It also ensures that excess glucose derived from food not needed for energy is put into body stores. However, in diabetic animals there is not enough insulin to switch off the liver's glucose production or to efficiently store excess glucose derived from foods. In diabetic dogs, the glucose may simply rampage through the blood stream (a condition known as hyperglycemia) without getting to the cells. Diabetic dogs can also suffer from hypoglycemia, a condition in which sugar levels drop radically. Hypoglycemic dogs appear confused, and they may even have a seizure. (If this happens, you can rub a bit of honey or syrup on the dog's gums).

As diabetes worsens, toxic ketones accumulate, causing vomiting, dehydration, and eventual death. Eventually, the kidneys let glucose leak into the urine. Signs of diabetes include:

- Excessive urination
- Increased appetite and thirst
- Weight loss
- Weakness
- Skin problems

If your Lab demonstrates any of these signs, take him to the vet immediately because untreated diabetes is fatal.

Diabetes can be managed (although not cured) with early diagnosis and proper treatment. It may be helpful to supplement your Lab's diet with an antioxidant such as vitamin E, which may minimize the breakdown of lipids in the body. Regular, moderate exercise is also important, as are regularly scheduled meals. (If you're away at mealtime, you can purchase a timed feeder set to the regular hour.)

Diabetic dogs will need regular doses of insulin, often twice a day. While some owners may be squeamish at first, the needles are so fine that your dog will probably not even notice the fact he is being given a shot. Remember to store the insulin in the refrigerator. When it comes time to give the shot, you will need to mix it by rolling (not shaking) the bottle gently in your hands. Draw the proper amount into the syringe and inject it subcutaneously under the scruff of the neck. Pull back on the plunger slightly to make sure you haven't hit a vein (you don't want to see blood) and then inject it.

Until recently, diabetic dogs had to rely on insulin used for human patients. However, a new formula designed specifically for animals, called Vetsulin (derived from pigs only), is now available. Vetsulin is more compatible with a dog's body chemistry.

Hypothyroidism

This common ailment in Labradors is characterized by the following:

- Cold intolerance
- Dry coat
- Lethargy
- Symmetrical, excess shedding
- Weight gain

In most cases, the cause is an immune-mediated disease in

Many diseases can be controlled with medication, allowing your Lab to live a normal life.

which the immune system somehow comes to the erroneous conclusion that the thyroid is a foreign body that should be done away with. Luckily, hypothyroidism is easily treatable with a thyroid replacement hormone, although it can't be cured.

Cushing's Disease (Hyperadrenocorticism)

With this condition, the adrenal gland overproduces corticosteroids. Signs include increased appetite and thirst, excessive urination, muscle wasting, and panting. The dog may have fluid accumulating in the abdomen. Cushing's can be treated either medically (through the use of several drug therapies) or with surgery.

Addison's Disease (Hypoadrenocorticism or Adrenocortical Insufficiency)

This very serious disorder occurs when the adrenal glands fail to secrete enough glucocorticoids and mineralocorticoids, hormones necessary for the regulation of electrolyte levels. It mostly occurs in middle-aged males. Signs include depression, weakness, vomiting, diarrhea, dehydration, weight loss, and shivering. Blood tests may show electrolyte imbalances of low sodium and chlorine and high potassium. A simple test called ACTH stimulation confirms the presence of the disease.

If left unnoticed or untreated, your dog will experience an "Addisonian crisis," in which his blood sugar will drop dangerously low and the imbalance of electrolytes will disrupt the heart rhythm. Untreated dogs usually die. Fortunately, this disease can be managed with medications. Treatment includes replacing the missing mineralocorticoid hormones. Your vet will be able to prescribe the right medication for your particular dog, but in any case he must remain on it for life. Common medications for Addison's include low-dose prednisone (to replace the cortisone). The aldosterone can be replaced with a daily oral medication or a monthly injectable medication. The injectable form is less expensive than the oral treatment, but neither is cheap. Addison's dogs need careful monitoring, and if they receive it, they can live a full and fairly normal life.

Eye Diseases

All breeds of dog can suffer from eye diseases, and Labs are no exception. In fact, they seem disposed to many eye conditions, including entropion of the lower eyelid, mild ectropion, medial canthal pocket syndrome, limbal melanoma, uveal cysts, canine anterior melanoma, cataracts, glaucoma, retinal atrophy (several types), optic nerve colobomas, and others. One of the most unusual, however, is focal retinal dysplasia and dwarfism.

Focal Retinal Dysplasia and Dwarfism

This unusual combination of genetic abnormalities is found mostly in certain field trial strains of Labradors. Retinal dysplasia, a congenital condition, is extremely common in field trial Labs by itself, with between 10 and 20 percent affected. Conformation lines are seldom affected. In retinal dysplasia, there is an abnormal development in which the retina develops folds instead of forming a thin membrane over the back of the eye. The fold becomes a blind spot. In mild cases, the dog still sees very well, and field dogs compensate by changing the way they hold their heads while marking a bird. However, some dogs have larger blind spots and significant visual impairment that may include retinal separation and cataracts.

In addition, some of these dogs also suffer from skeletal dysplasia that results in short-limbed dwarfism. It has been suggested that this condition is inherited as one autosomal gene that has recessive effects on the skeleton and incomplete dominant effects on the eye.

Some Labs contract only mild retinal dysplasia. It is imperative for breeders of field trial Labs to have their dogs checked for this condition, though, so that it is not passed on. Unfortunately, the mild form is hard to diagnose, because small eye folds can "straighten out." As the dog matures, the condition becomes virtually unnoticeable, although the dog is still, of course, a carrier for the condition. Your own veterinarian will not be able to detect the small folds, although specialists who perform CERF (Canine Eye Registry Foundation) exams can detect them using special tools. The most reliable eye exams for this disease can be performed on puppies between the ages of 6 weeks and 6 months, with 14 weeks being the optimal time. This exam also finds cases of retinal folds that fade later in the dog's life.

A second form of retinal dysplasia is found mostly in Labradors

Eye Witness

By knowing what to expect and working with your breeder and veterinarian, you can give your Lab the best chance to have healthy eyes for his lifetime—and chances are good that he will. As always, you are your dog's first line of defense. Anything unusual should be cause for concern and reason for a veterinary visit.

of European ancestry; this form is caused by a recessive gene and affects only the vision (with no attached dwarfism). A dog who inherits both genes will become blind; a dog who inherits one from only one parent will have normal or only slightly impaired vision. There is no treatment for this disease.

Progressive Retinal Atrophy (PRA)

Progressive Retinal Atrophy (PRA) is an inherited, nonpainful disease of the retina that can be prevented with proper genetic screening. The retina, located inside the back of the eye, contains specialized cells called photoreceptors that absorb the light focused on them. The photoreceptors then convert the light into electrical nerve signals, which are passed by the optic nerve to the brain. The retinal photoreceptors are specialized into rods for vision in dim light (night vision) and cones for vision in bright light (day and color vision). PRA usually damages the rods first and then the cones of both eyes at once, so night blindness may be the first sign of the disease. Human beings get the same disease, but it is called retinitis pigmentosa.

Labs are disposed to a variety of eye diseases, including entropion of the lower eyelid, cataracts, glaucoma, and retinal atrophy.

Affected dogs will adapt to their handicap as long as their environment remains constant and they are not faced with situations requiring excellent vision. You may notice the pupils of their eyes remain dilated, and increased reflectivity of the eye will cause a noticeable shininess. At the same time, the lens of the eyes may become cloudy or opaque, perhaps even resulting in a cataract. Your vet can diagnose PRA using eye drops and an instrument called an indirect ophthalmoscope. Unfortunately, there is no cure, but some vets believe that specific oral antioxidant therapy can slow it down. On average, a dog becomes blind within six months.

Blindness

Blindness is a rather common affliction of dogs. It can be caused by glaucoma, corneal problems, cancer, trauma, retinal diseases, or cataracts. Blind dogs require some extra care but can enjoy long and full lives. It is not the tragedy for them that it is for humans, and in point of fact, blindness seems to bother dog owners more than it does dogs, who live in a universe filled with rich smells and vibrant sounds.

If you are patient with your blind dog, conservative about moving furniture around, and willing to make a few adjustments to his new lifestyle, there's no reason why he can't go on happily for many years more.

Don't baby your blind dog. He'll still enjoy walks and being outside in your company. Of course, you should not leave him alone outside. Talk to him, give him squeaky toys, and try in every way to enrich his world of sound and smell. Give him time and he will learn to navigate around your house. In fact, if the blindness has been coming on gradually, he may have already learned to do this so well that it may come as a surprise to you to discover he's blind! Be consistent about his feeding and sleeping areas, and speak to him before touching him. Make sure you don't clip off his whiskers, which he can use as little guides around the rooms. I know of one dog who carried a stuffed toy in his mouth and used it as a "bumper." In fact, you can purchase a harness-like device that acts much in the same way, although most dogs seem preternaturally able to guide themselves.

You should also help your dog by remaining very conscious of open doors, fireplaces, hot tubs, and sharp objects located at your Labrador's eye level. Put a note on his collar that states he is blind in the event he becomes lost.

Senior Labs may begin to lose or completely lose their eyesight. This is disorienting for them, though they can still get around. If your dog has limited or no vision, be careful about rearranging furniture or making other changes. You want the environment to be as familiar as possible for him.

Cataracts

Labradors can also be affected by cataracts. A cataract appears white or gray. It usually begins as a small dot and then progresses to include larger areas of the lens. If a large portion of the lens is occluded, the dog's vision will be affected, but not all cataracts lead to blindness. Cataracts may develop in one or both eyes. If you suspect your Lab has developed a cataract, a visit to a veterinary ophthalmologist is in order.

There is no medical treatment known to slow the progression of, prevent, or reverse cataract development. The only current treatment (for both humans and dogs) is surgery to remove the cataract. This surgery is usually offered only to patients who have developed the disease in both eyes. The technique is called phacoemulsification and involves using ultrasonic waves to destroy the cataract. (Despite the common terminology "laser surgery," no lasers are involved!) Your vet is the best one to help you make a decision about this option for your Lab.

Gastrointestinal Disorders

While many conditions cause gastrointestinal difficulties, you always need to consider the possibility that your dog has eaten something he shouldn't. Labradors are famous for eating non-food items, including balls, corncobs, and string. These things can get stuck anywhere along the intestinal tract. Smaller objects may make it through the stomach but lodge in the small intestine; larger objects can get caught in the stomach itself. Strings and yarn are especially dangerous, because they can block large sections of the intestine. Even worse, the string can tighten and actually cut through the intestinal wall, sometimes in several places.

A blockage in the intestines is an emergency. In addition to vomiting (or attempted vomiting) and diarrhea, a dog with a blockage may have a fever. Your vet can check for a blockage with x-rays (sometimes using barium for contrast). She may, however, need to do exploratory surgery—many soft objects, like socks, don't show up well on x-rays. If a foreign object appears on the x-ray, the vet will probably need to remove it surgically, although in a few cases, a little petroleum jelly or a similar substance will help it through if it is lodged in the large intestine.

Labradors are famous for eating non-food items, so be sure to supervise your dog carefully, and provide him with plenty of appropriate chew toys.

Straining and Constipation

Straining is often caused by a large bowel infection, especially when the stool is covered with mucus, blood, or liquid. Parasites, bacteria, viruses, or stress can also be a factor. "Normal" constipation is characterized by a dry, hard stool and may indicate prostate trouble or something that's stuck (like a bone) somewhere in the intestines. If your dog has constipation for more than a day or so, check with your vet. In a worst-case scenario, surgery may be required.

In many cases, straining may not be a sign of constipation; instead, it may be a sign of colitis (inflammation of the bowels). Dogs seldom have primary constipation, but when it occurs the stool is hard. When colitis occurs, the stools are soft.

Diarrhea

Diarrhea is a sign of a disease rather than a disease in and of itself, and diarrhea that includes blood or mucus is especially worrisome. The main reason for diarrhea is "dietary indiscretion," a fancy way of saying that your dog has been eating something he shouldn't. Other causes include parasites, infection, foreign bodies, inflammatory bowel disease, pancreatitis, and liver disease.

If your Lab is suffering from diarrhea, the first thing you should do is place him on a fast for 24 hours but allow water. Follow with a bland diet of boiled meat and rice. If the diarrhea continues for a day or two after a 24-hour fast, a trip to the vet is in order.

For simple diarrhea, Kaopectate (about 2cc/kg every 4-6 hours) or Pepto-Bismol (2cc/kg every 4-6 hours) administered orally may be helpful. Herbalists often use slippery elm with good effect.

Bloody Stools

Blood can appear in your dog's stools in several different ways, and each kind suggests a different problem. So while it's not fun to stare at your dog's leavings, doing so can give you and your vet important clues about a possible disease condition. For instance:

- Black, tarry stools indicate bleeding high up in the digestive tract and may suggest a bleeding stomach ulcer.
- Reddish stools suggest something lower down, perhaps intestinal ulcers or ulcerative colitis.
- Red-streaked stools that are otherwise normal in appearance can indicate bleeding in the last segment of the large intestine, possibly ulcerative colitis or another bowel disease.

Changes in stool color can also signify digestive problems. If you find blood in your Lab's stool, take a sample to your vet for a further look.

Vomiting

Dogs vomit easily, which is fortunate because they are in the habit of eating the most disgusting things. Vomiting, then, is a

A Homeopathic Remedy

For those who follow homeopathy, a standard remedy for diarrhea is Pulsatilla (30c) if there is a yellow stool or if the quality of the stool changes from stool to stool, or Arsenicum (30c) if the dog has gotten into something awful. These doses can be given orally, with one dose administered every few hours. Give no more than three doses, however.

Many times you will see the suffix "itis" as part of a diagnosis. This suffix just means "inflammation of." Thus, "pancreatitis" is the inflammation of the pancreas, "colitis" is the inflammation of the colon, and "tonsillitis" is an inflammation of the tonsils.

survivalist tool they've used successfully for millennia. Young animals are especially prone to finding non-edible things to eat, eating them, and then throwing them up. With older animals, vomiting is more likely to be a sign of kidney, gastrointestinal, or liver problems.

If your dog vomits, withhold food for about 12 hours to give his system a rest. Follow with a bland diet of boiled meat and rice. If there's nothing seriously wrong, most dogs will "come around" after that time. You can treat simple vomiting at home with Kaopectate or Pepto-Bismol at 2 cc/kg every 4-6 hours.

You should worry about your dog vomiting if you believe he's been exposed to some poison or garbage, especially if he seems ill or depressed afterward and expresses no interest in further eating. Repeated episodes can also be a cause for concern. Take your dog to the vet if vomiting does not cease within a day and a half.

Kidney (Renal) Disease

The kidneys serve many critical bodily functions: They filter and remove toxins through the urine, regulate calcium and vitamin D levels, maintain fluid levels, and secrete a special hormone that controls red blood cell production. Unfortunately, after cancer, kidney disease is a leading cause of death in dogs. Simple old age is one cause of kidney failure, but other causes include bacterial and viral infections, nutritional factors, immune system deficits, toxins, and inherited disorders.

As dogs grow older, their chances of developing kidney problems increase. Besides old age, other factors leading to kidney disease include:

- Amyloidosis (caused by abnormal deposits of a certain protein in the kidney)
- Autoimmune diseases
- Cancer
- Congenital and inherited disorders
- Inflammation
- Parasites
- Toxic reaction to poisons or medications
- Trauma
- Viral, bacterial, or fungal infections

Dogs with kidney disease can show a variety of physical signs. Some of the signs are nonspecific and may be seen in other disorders such as liver or pancreatic diseases, or urinary tract disorders not involving the kidneys. Signs may include:

- Bad breath
- Changes in urine quality or volume
- Diarrhea
- Hunched-over posture or reluctance to move
- Increased water consumption
- Lack of appetite and weight loss
- Lethargy
- Pale gums
- Poor hair coat
- Swelling of the abdomen
- Vomiting

Laboratory tests can confirm the diagnosis, and treatment depends upon whether the disease is occurring suddenly (acute) or occurring over a period of several months (chronic).

Acute Kidney Disease

Acute kidney disease can be caused by infection, parasites, or exposure to toxins. Dogs with acute kidney disease may vomit, lose their appetite, develop a fever, and undergo changes in urination. Early, aggressive treatment may be able to reverse the disease. Your vet will determine the cause and begin intravenous fluid therapy and possibly other medications to reduce nausea and get the kidneys working properly. If needed, some clinics are able to perform kidney dialysis, and a few can even perform kidney transplants!

Chronic Kidney Disease

In chronic cases, dogs can have irreversible lesions in the kidneys, but you probably won't be aware of it until most of the kidneys' function is gone, something that may take years. Many older dogs suffer from some degree of kidney damage, and owners need to make sure these animals always have access to plenty of fresh, clean water. Some dogs may need added potassium or other electrolytes. Dogs with kidney damage should be put on a

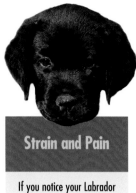

diet of reduced, high-quality protein. Your vet can supply you with a special commercial diet for this purpose. You may also want to supplement with water-soluble B and C vitamins.

Urinary Tract Problems

Urinary tract problems are common in Labradors, with females at particular risk. Symptoms include straining and excessive urination. Get a urine sample and take it to your vet. The best way to accomplish this is to attach a small (very small) paper cup to the end of a stretched-out wire clothes hanger or other piece of wire. That way you won't have to stand right next to the dog. (Most dogs stop urinating when you try to put a cup underneath them.)

Infections of the urinary tract are treated with a course of antibiotics. In some cases, your vet will recommend a dietary supplement like cranberry juice or capsules to acidify the urinary tract.

Bladder Stones

Labradors, especially males, can also develop bladder stones (urolithiasis) anywhere in the urinary tract, but about 85 percent of the time in the bladder itself. Dogs with bladder stones may have blood in their urine; they may also urinate frequently but pass only a small amount each time. They often strain while urinating, although some dogs show no outward signs at all.

There are several types of bladder stones, with silica stones more common in this breed than in some others. All bladder stones are formed the same way: as tiny crystals that precipitate out of the urine, eventually coming together and growing larger and larger. No one knows why some dogs get them and some do not, but most researchers believe it's a combination of heredity, bacterial infections, diet, and urine pH. Depending on the specific case, dogs can be treated medically or surgically. (It's an easy surgical procedure.) Changing the diet is appropriate in some cases, but follow the advice of your veterinarian.

Liver Disease

The liver is the largest internal organ in the body, but the warning signs that appear when something goes wrong can be vague. Lack of appetite, vomiting, diarrhea, weight loss, and lethargy signal so many diseases besides liver problems that further tests are necessary. To make things even more complicated, while sometimes the problem can indeed stem primarily from the liver, very often the original disease comes from a different source, including medications or poisons that affect the liver only secondarily.

Signs of liver disease include:
- Abdominal pain
- Excess drinking and urination
- Intermittent and recurrent gastrointestinal upsets, including vomiting, diarrhea, and constipation
- Jaundiced eyes or belly skin
- Lethargy that becomes worse
- Behavioral changes
- Orange or dark-yellow urine
- Pale feces
- Swollen abdomen
- Weight loss

The earlier liver problems are identified, the better the chances for recovery. The liver can regenerate to some extent if there is not a lot of scarring (cirrhosis). The more scarring on the liver, the more difficult it is for the liver to do its work.

Grooming time is the perfect opportunity to check for lumps and bumps on your Labrador.

To help prevent liver problems, avoid feeding your dog a raw diet, and be careful when giving him treats. Treats made of animal by-products can be dicey, especially stuff that is imported from places like Thailand, where control over such products is practically nonexistent. In addition, carefully monitor your pet when he is being medicated for any reason, as many drugs can tax the liver. All dogs, especially older ones, should have yearly bloodwork to test for liver and kidney problems.

The following are some of the most common liver disorders affecting Labradors.

Chronic Hepatitis (Inflammation of the Liver)

Chronic hepatitis affects those dogs who are middle-aged and older, and Labradors are one of the most commonly affected

breeds. This disease can be caused by a virus or bacteria, but it can also be a drug- or immune-mediated response. Certain toxins can also be responsible. Hepatitis can also be a secondary result from inflammatory bowel disease, pancreatitis, and infections. Most of the time, your vet won't know what originally caused the disease but will work to treat it with medications and special diets.

Bathing and grooming your Lab regularly will allow you to monitor any irregular lumps or bumps on your dog.

Liver Tumors

Liver tumors affect older dogs. If the tumor in non-cancerous, it can be removed, with a very good prognosis. If the tumor is malignant, however, the prognosis is extremely poor. You vet will use blood panels, ultrasound, x-rays, and biopsies to determine the nature of the tumor. Several types of biopsy are available, all of which require general anesthesia, but some are more invasive than others. However, a biopsy is an important tool your vet can use to determine exactly what the problem in the liver is.

Lumps and Bumps

You may be grooming your Labrador and all of a sudden notice a lump on the skin. Is this a harmless "skin tag" or a fatal malignancy? Could it be something in between? (Some lumps that are benign at first can turn malignant.) Benign lumps include sebaceous cysts, hair follicle cysts, folliculitis, warts, sebaceous hyperkeratosis, and epulis (in the mouth). Malignant lumps include mast cell tumors, basal cell tumors, skin cancer of the lymph nodes, lymphomas, and melanomas.

Lumps are some of the most common and scariest signs that can appear on your Lab. If a lump suddenly appears on your dog, the best thing for you to do is to have it evaluated by your vet, if only for your own peace of mind. Try to note down everything you have noticed about the lump to report. The following are some things to consider:

- Where is the lump? Lumps in the mammary or lymph tissues are usually more dangerous, as are deep-seated lumps.
- Is the lump painful or itchy? Has the dog been licking at it?

These things suggest a bite or some other trauma.

- How long has the lump been there? New, rapidly growing lumps are very suspicious.
- Is the lump hard or soft, and how is it attached? Hard lumps that seem to be attached to the bone are very suspicious.

Further examination may require a fine needle aspirate, in which the vet inserts a small-bore needle into the lump and withdraws some of its contents. The material is smeared onto a slide and examined under a microscope. If the tissue is too dense for this kind of examination, your vet may need to take a biopsy of the lump or perhaps remove the entire lump and send it off to a pathology lab. This requires general anesthesia.

Nervous System Disorders

The nervous system is, as the name indicates, the system that controls your dog's nerve impulses. It also gathers information about the environment through specialized nerve endings in the skin. The resulting sensations are touch, pressure, pain, and heat and cold (thermoreceptors).

Canine Cognitive Dysfunction (CCD)

According to Pfizer Pharmaceutical, 62 percent of dogs aged ten years and older may develop signs of canine cognitive dysfunction

Lethargy is a sign that your Labrador may not be feeling well.

(CCD). These include:

- Confusion or disorientation. (The dog may get lost in his own back yard or become trapped in corners or behind furniture.)
- Forgetting housetraining abilities.
- Maintaining lower levels of activity.
- Not recognizing people or other pets.
- Pacing, lying awake all night, or changes in sleeping patterns.
- Staring vaguely into space.

Luckily, there is medication available that can successfully treat this condition. Talk to your vet to discover your options.

Epilepsy

Epilepsy is an inherited condition in Labs that develops between one and seven years of age. This pup is still free from any signs or symptoms.

It is strongly suspected that epilepsy is inherited in Labrador Retrievers. In dogs who suffer from epilepsy, there is abnormal electrical activity in the brain that interferes with nerve transmission. The dog cannot use his muscles properly during the seizure, resulting in involuntary contractions of the muscles that compose a seizure. The first seizure usually occurs between one and seven years of age.

Primary epilepsy is a condition characterized by seizures of unknown (idiopathic) origin. When it is known what is causing the seizures, the disease is referred to as secondary epilepsy, which can be caused by such things as hypoglycemia (low blood sugar), liver problems, poisoning, heart problems, infection, and cancer. Blood tests, x-rays, electrocardiograms, ultrasounds, MRIs, and other tests may rule out these other conditions.

A classic epileptic event has several stages. The first stage, or aura, precedes the event itself. During this stage, the dog may try to hide from or stay very close to the owner; he may even become aggressive.

The seizure itself is called the ictus or crisis stage. A seizure is a scary event to observe, one that is even more distressing to the owner than to the dog. In a generalized seizure (tonic-clonic), all of the skeletal muscles contract, and the dog loses consciousness. He will fall to his side with his head thrown back and legs stretched out. He may vocalize, twitch, urinate, defecate, or drool. This part of the seizure is called the tonic phase. In the clonic phase, which usually occurs right after the tonic phase, the dog will jerk rhythmically (perhaps look like he's running) and clench his jaws. During the crisis, or ictus, take care to prevent the dog from hurting himself. Remove furniture in close proximity to your pet, and prevent the animal from falling downstairs. Do not try to put your hands in his mouth, as you can be bitten very badly. The best thing you can do for your dog at this time is to be quiet, dim the room if you can, and keep other pets away. Time the seizure and keep records. Call your vet after it is over to ask for an appointment and consultation.

During the post-ictal period, the dog will lie quite still and then get up, usually showing some aftereffects of the seizure, such as disorientation or passing out. Unfortunately, this phase can last for hours or even longer. In between episodes, the pet will appear normal, both physically and mentally. Not all seizures are so dramatic, though. In a partial seizure, only a part of the body, such as the head, may be affected. A partial seizure probably has a specific cause, unlike many cases of generalized epilepsy.

Many drugs are available to control epilepsy, although the disease has no cure and treatment is for life. The goal of drug therapy is to reduce the intensity, frequency, and duration of the seizures. By giving the appropriate medication at the right dosage, the condition will be well controlled in most pets.

Rabies Alert

You will need to make sure throughout your Lab's lifetime that he is safely vaccinated against rabies. Labs meet all kinds of critters in their outdoor adventures, so protecting against rabies is absolutely necessary.

Rabies

Rabies is a deadly neurological viral disease transmitted through the bite of an infected animal. Getting a rabies vaccination for your dog is not only safe and sensible, it is mandatory everywhere in the United States. Puppies should be immunized against this disease between 16 and 24 weeks of age.

Skeletal Diseases

Without a skeleton that functions properly, your dog isn't going anywhere. As a result, diseases of this vital system are a cause for concern.

Hip Dysplasia

This complex disease is an inherited condition that tends to be more common among larger dogs, like Labradors. It can show up in varying degrees—from mild to completely crippling. The easiest way to think of hip dysplasia is as a kind of "joint looseness." In

Senior Labs can still lead active, normal lives with the proper care.

dogs who suffer from this disease, the femoral head does not fit snugly into the socket. Symptoms may include difficulty in getting up, stiffness, "bunny hopping," reluctance to climb stairs, and restricted movement in the hind legs. Only an x-ray can definitively detect the disease.

Many treatment options exist for hip dysplasia, including pectineal myotomy (a relatively minor muscle-cutting surgery that achieves results in many cases without loss of movement). However, this procedure does not treat the disease or improve anatomic function of the joint. For the majority of dogs, it only provides temporary relief of pain, which generally recurs within six to nine months. Basically, it does not alter the progression of the disease or cure it. Other options include femoral head osteotomy (removal of part of the ball of the joint that is used more in smaller dogs); triple pelvic osteotomy (this expensive treatment can be performed only if arthritic damage to the joint has not yet occurred; the pelvis is cut in three pieces and the hip rotated); and total hip replacement. Each of these procedures has its place in the surgical arsenal against hip dysplasia. You can determine in consultation with your vet which procedure, if any, is right for your dog.

Drug treatments include buffered aspirin (which alleviates pain but can cause gastric ulcers), steroids (which works wonders against the pain but can actually worsen the condition), and non-steroidal anti-inflammatory drugs (NSAIDS). These drugs are much safer than aspirin but can cause adverse effects in some animals. Nutraceutical supplements, which are categorized not exactly as drugs and not exactly as food (but somewhere in the middle), also show great promise. Chief among them is a combination of glucosamine and chondroitin. Because the nutraceutical market is not well regulated, it's often best to follow your veterinarian's advice. Other nutraceuticals, including antioxidants, may also be beneficial, and some companies are now experimenting with combining glucosamine, chondroitin, and antioxidants in a new formula.

Arthritis

As our dogs live longer lives, they are at increased risk of developing arthritis. About 20 percent of all adult dogs have arthritis to some degree, and obese individuals who carry the most weight are more likely to be affected. For dogs (and people), the most common type of arthritis is osteoarthritis, which results from damaged cartilage. Because cartilage doesn't have nerves, the dog feels no pain and continues to be active. This only accelerates the damage. Signs of arthritis include:

- Avoidance of activity
- Limping
- Reluctance to get up or climb stairs
- Sensitivity to cold and damp weather
- Shrinking away from being touched
- Stiffness

Arthritis can be more troublesome to dogs than blindness or deafness, but we have ways to combat it. Many new medications can make a positive difference in your dog's life. Nutraceuticals, a new class of supplements between regular drugs and traditional herbal preparations, offer important benefits to arthritic dogs. Examples include glucosamine and chondroitin. Glucosamine is a cartilage-protective nutraceutical, while chondroitin sulfate is an important glycoaminoglycan (GAG) that binds water in the cartilage matrix. Adding both glucosamine and chondroitin sulfate in a single supplement is a great way to help your pet heal himself. These supplements are not simply "pain-killers." Their direct effect is to be both protective and restorative, leading to less pain and more mobility. This, in turn, will have an important effect on your dog's attitude. It is important to remember, however, that unlike traditional drug therapy, nutraceuticals work slowly (six to eight weeks), and not all dogs respond. Make sure you buy a high-quality supplement, as not all are created equal. Check with your veterinarian as well before buying something over the counter.

Be alert to signs that your older Lab may be experiencing joint pain.

Other treatments that have been found to be effective against arthritis include physical therapy, Chinese or Japanese acupuncture, chiropractic treatment, and even gene therapy. There's a whole new world out there for arthritis sufferers, and your logy, creaky, slow-to-get-up and hesitant-to-climb-stairs dog may get a new lease on life with one of the many new treatments available. So far, though, there is

no real cure for arthritis—only relief from its more debilitating effects. In addition to veterinary care, you can make your Labrador more comfortable at home by supplying extra bedding and a snug place by the fire or hot air vent.

CANINE EMERGENCIES

Dogs can get into trouble really quickly. Part of the reason is because they tend to "hide" signs of illness. Their wild ancestors knew that a weak, sick dog could be preyed upon by stronger animals, so they wisely didn't pass this information on to their rivals. Today's dogs are equally wary about cluing us in to the fact that they don't feel well, and by the time we notice something, the dog has probably been ill for longer than we think. Here are some of the main signs that something might be seriously wrong with your dog and that a veterinary opinion is in order:

- Bleeding from the nose, mouth, rectum, or genitalia.
- Difficulty breathing.
- Drinking excessively.
- Inability to eat or drink without vomiting.
- Inability to urinate or defecate or showing signs of stress when attempting these activities.
- Lethargy.
- Not eating or eating much less than normal for more than one day.
- Pain when you touch or move the animal.
- Pale gums.

Bee, Wasp, and Hornet Stings

While all stings are painful, some are deadly. If your dog is allergic to bee stings, he may have trouble breathing and develop hives. Give him an antihistamine and take him to the vet right away. If he does not seem to be having an allergic reaction, scrape out the stinger with a credit card. (Don't try pulling it out, because you can squeeze in more poison.) Apply a cold compress and meat tenderizer to the wound. Call your veterinarian if an infection develops.

Bleeding

If your Lab is bleeding profusely, first apply pressure. Don't stop for at least five minutes. Place one bandage on top of another as the first becomes soaked with blood. Don't remove the old bandage, because you may pull off a forming clot. It is best to use a sterile bandage, of course, but if you don't have one handy (and in serious cases, you probably won't), use anything. Use towels, rags, old shirts, bare hands—whatever it takes to stop the bleeding. You'll be taking the dog to the vet anyway, and he'll administer any needed antibiotics.

Much more serious than regular cuts, of course, are cuts that slice across arteries. Arterial blood is usually very bright red and comes in spurts, rather than the steady flow of darker blood characteristic of surface or venous cuts. In case of arterial bleeding, you must stop the blood flow at once. Apply strong pressure to the blood flow. If the bleeding continues, apply pressure to the pressure point closest to the wound, between the wound and the heart. Pressure points are located in "armpits," the groin, and just below the base on the underside of the tail. Press firmly until the bleeding slows. You will have to relax the pressure for a few seconds every few minutes so that you don't cause tissue and nerve death.

Bloat

The technical name for this terrible condition is gastric dilatation volvulus (GDV). When a dog is afflicted with bloat, gases or air build up in the stomach, typically after a large meal. The technical name for this expansion is dilatation, but "bloat" says it all. After a certain point, the stomach twists more than 180 degrees on its long axis (this is called torsion), cutting off contact with the esophagus and trapping the gas so the dog can't belch or pass gas. This puts pressure on the large blood vessels of the abdomen, leading ultimately to organ failure. The stomach may even rupture. In addition, digestion ceases at this point, causing fermenting food and bacteria to accumulate in the stomach, causing tissue death. The food and bacteria can even get into the blood stream, forming clots and perhaps pushing the dog into shock. *Dogs of any breed can get bloat, including Labradors.*

This disease attacks suddenly and often at night. A stricken dog can die within two hours of onset, and more than one owner has come

Bloat is a life-threatening illness that occurs when a dog's stomach fills with gas and twists. What exactly sets off a case of bloat has not been determined, but conscientious owners do what they can to prevent it by keeping their dogs at the proper weight; making sure dogs who get stressed when they eat are fed in calm areas; feeding well-rounded meals; and feeding more than once a day.

home to the tragic sight of a dog killed by bloat. It is an agonizing and painful death. Symptoms of bloat include:

- Unsuccessful attempts to vomit
- Extended abdomen in most cases as the condition progresses
- Pacing and discomfort
- Pale mucous membranes
- Panting
- Repeatedly lying down and getting back up
- Salivation

These signs indicate an emergency. Get your Lab to the emergency vet clinic immediately, even if it's 3:00 a.m. *Do not wait.* If left untreated even for a few hours, your dog will probably die. The first 20 minutes to half an hour are most critical. If you arrive at the animal hospital in time, the vet may be able to insert a tube down the dog's stomach to release the gases if torsion has not occurred. (This can be confirmed by an x-ray.) The dog will be treated for shock and made ready for surgery. If torsion has occurred, the vet may insert a tube directly through the abdominal wall into the stomach. Once the situation is stabilized, the vet will perform surgery to reposition the stomach.

Gastropexy is the treatment of choice when a dog is subjected to one or more bouts of bloat. In this surgical procedure, the vet will stitch the stomach to the abdominal wall in an attempt to prevent it from twisting. This procedure will not stop bloat, but it will prevent the accompanying torsion. Even the best treatment does not assure success, though. Animals who have a lot of dead tissue or who have suffered cardiac complications are at increased risk of death or at least a long and difficult recovery.

No one really knows what causes bloat or how to prevent it. Many factors combine to create a risk environment for the disease. They include breed, size and shape of the dog, age, genetics, diet, and (rather surprisingly) personality.

- Age: The older the dog, the higher the risk.
- Gender: Male dogs have a *slightly* increased risk.
- Personality: Fearful, nervous, and aggressive dogs have the highest risk for bloat; low-key, happy, easygoing dogs the least. Dogs eating in a stressed environment are at increased risk.
- Weight: Underweight dogs are most at risk. Researchers believe that chronic underweight may indicate a permanent

problem with the gastrointestinal system that leads to the disease.

- Fast Eating: Gobblers are at a much higher risk of bloat. This is probably because they gulp air. If your Lab is a fast eater, try placing a rock or heavy object in the middle of his food dish to force him to slow down as he eats around it.
- Genetics: Dogs with close relatives who have had bloat are at threefold increased risk.
- Food Type: Dogs fed solely on dry food are at increased risk of bloat. Dogs fed with table scraps or even water added are at lower risk.
- Feeding Schedule: Dogs fed only once a day are at greater risk of bloat. The more frequently you feed your dog, the lower the risk.
- Flatulence or Belching: Belching dogs have an 80 percent increased risk of bloat. Flatulent dogs are at a 20 percent increased risk.

Fish Hook Emergency

Labradors were bred to be fishing partners, but this doesn't mean they are safety conscious when it comes to fish hooks (or lines)! If the hook is caught in the mouth, your vet can give him a short-acting sedative and snip off the barb and remove the hook. Things are more serious if the hook winds up in the esophagus. If you even think your dog has swallowed a hook, don't pull on the line; that will only serve to "set the hook" and make things worse. A hook caught in the esophagus requires the vet to insert an endoscope down the throat and use special instruments to remove it. On occasion, surgery may be required. If the dog swallows the fishing line, it's another kind of emergency. The line will ball up inside the stomach and be carried into the intestine, where it can actually saw through the intestines and kill the animal. Please be cautious and keep all fishing equipment away from your dog.

Remember that even the hardiest Lab can suffer frostbite if overexposed to frigid temperatures.

Frostbite

Bitter weather can give even your sturdy Lab frostbite on the toes or ears. Signs include pale or gray skin and reddened ear tips. If frostbite occurs, submerge the afflicted areas in warm (not hot) water. Don't rub the paws or ears; that will only increase the

First-Aid Kit for Dogs

You don't need a special box; anything handy will do, but a fishing tackle box works very well. On the outside of the box, write "Dog First-Aid Kit" in bold letters. Put it in an obvious place, because someone other than you might need to find it. To the inside of the box lid, attach any special information someone might need to know about any conditions or allergic reactions your Lab may have. Tape a special card with the name, address, and phone number of your vet. Also, write down the use and dosage for each medication your dog is likely to need now, so you won't have to try to figure it out during an emergency. The first-aid kit is also a good place to keep a copy of your dog's medical records, including his rabies certificate.

If you have a chance, take a course in first aid. Sometimes special clinics are given in first aid for animals. It is very helpful to learn to perform artificial respiration, mouth-to-mouth resuscitation, and the Heimlich maneuver. You never know when you might need them for animals or people.

You should include the following items in the ultimate canine first-aid kit:

- Activated charcoal (for poisoning)
- Aloe vera (for minor burns)
- Antibiotic cream
- Antibiotic soap (skin and wound cleanser)
- Baking soda (for burns caused by acids)
- Bandages
- Benadryl (1-2 mg per lb every eight hours; 2-4 25mg tablets every eight hours)
- Betadine (treating wounds)
- Canine first-aid manual
- Canine rectal thermometer
- Clinging wrap heat or ice pack
- Epsom salts (soaking wounds, especially on the feet)
- Eye dropper
- Gauze and cotton pads (to clean and cover wounds)
- Gentle eye wash
- Hydrocortisone cream (minor inflammation)
- Ipecac or 3 percent hydrogen peroxide (to induce vomiting)
- Kaopectate for diarrhea (1 mg per 15 lbs 1-2 times a day, or 1 tbsp for every 10 pounds every six hours)
- Magnifying glass
- Milk of magnesia (for constipation—administer with equal amounts of mineral oil)
- Mineral oil (numerous uses, including constipation)
- Pepto-Bismol (digestive upsets and diarrhea; 1 tsp per 5 lbs during a six-hour period)
- Petroleum jelly (numerous uses)
- Round-tip scissors
- Rubber or latex gloves (to protect hands and prevent contamination of wounds)
- Saline eye solution and artificial tear gel
- Soft muzzle (injured dogs tend to bite)
- Styptic powder (stops minor bleeding)
- Syringe (without needle—to administer oral medication)
- Thermal blanket (prevents shock by preserving the dog's body heat)
- Tweezers or hemostat
- Vinegar (for burns caused by alkaloids)
- Witch hazel (insect bites, minor injuries)

irritation. When they feel warm again, your dog is probably out of danger.

Heat Exhaustion or Stroke

Labradors are cold-weather dogs; heat is their enemy. Remember that humans are tropical beasts, and what's fun exercise for us at a balmy 80°F can be life-threatening to your Labrador.

Leaving your dog in a closed car, even with the window cracked,

is a very dangerous proposition. As the dog continues to pant, the air inside the car becomes even warmer and more saturated with moisture, making it more and more difficult for the dog to cool down.

Black Labs are at the highest risk for heatstroke or exhaustion.

Black Labs are at the highest degree of risk for heatstroke or exhaustion; that coat really soaks up the sun! When it is humid, dogs are even more at risk, because effective evaporation of the water on their tongues can't occur. If the body temperature exceeds 106°F, cellular function is seriously impaired. Unconsciousness and even death may follow.

Signs of heat stroke include fast breathing or panting, a bright-red tongue, and bright-red mucous membranes.

If your dog is suffering from heat stroke, you'll need to cool him down as fast as possible. First, bring him to a cool, shaded area. Then, if he is in shock, administer CPR. Hose him down with cool water and put cool, wet towels around his neck. Soak his feet in water or rub them with alcohol. Do not use cold water, however; that has the effect of restricting the capillary blood flow and shutting in the heat. Finally, get the dog to the vet in an air-conditioned car as soon as possible.

Inability to Breathe

Dogs who have stopped breathing may respond to cardiopulmonary resuscitation (CPR), and to be effective, it must be administered quickly. When performing CPR, you are giving your dog artificial respiration and chest compressions to get his heart going at the same time. If possible, it's best to have two people working: one for the breathing and one for the heart. Of course, that's not always possible. The chances of its success aren't great, but it is better than nothing. Also, no national standards for canine CPR exist, so guidelines vary.

A dog who needs CPR will be unconscious. You cannot perform CPR on a conscious dog. For one thing, it's ineffective and dangerous for the dog. For another, you'll be bitten.

CPR works using the ABC method: airway, breathing, and circulation.

"A" Is for Airway

If your dog is not breathing, the first thing you need to do is to establish a clear airway.

Carefully pull the tongue out of the animal's mouth. Use gloves—a dog who is almost unconscious may bite instinctively. Bring the head in line with the neck, but don't pull if there is trauma to the neck area. Visually inspect to see if the airway is open. If you see a foreign body, put your finger in the back of the mouth above the tongue and sweep the object upward. If the object remains stuck, lift the dog upside down with his back to your chest, and give several sharp thrusts just below the dog's rib cage to expel it.

Close the mouth and do two rescue breaths (your mouth to his nose). If you are able to breathe into the nose with no obstructions, go to B. If you encounter problems, reposition the neck and look down the throat for foreign bodies. If you see any, reach in and attempt to extract them. If that doesn't work, try the Heimlich maneuver: pick up the hind legs, holding your dog upside down, with his back against your chest. With your arms, give the dog five sharp thrusts to the abdomen to expel the object.

"B" Is for Breathing

Look and listen for signs of breathing. If there are none, place your hands around the dog's muzzle to prevent air from escaping through the side of the mouth, and breathe forcefully into the nostrils. The chest should *expand and fall* if you are getting air into the lungs. Rescue breathing should be given at a rate of eight to ten breaths per minute (or one breath every six seconds). Get your dog to the vet as soon as possible after he is breathing on his own.

If you think your pet has been poisoned, call your vet or the ASPCA National Animal Poison Control Center at (900) 443-0000 immediately. The charge is billed directly to the caller's phone. You can also call (888) 4ANI-HELP ((888) 426-4435), billed to the caller's credit card only. Follow-up calls can be made for no additional charge by dialing (888) 299-2973.

"C" Is for Circulation

If there is no pulse, place the dog on a hard surface with his right side down. Use the heel of your hand to compress the chest on the lower side right behind the elbow. The compression should be firm and not a sudden blow. It helps to have two people: the first gives the cardiac massage, while the second does the breathing. CPR should be given at a rate of 80 to 120 compressions per minute, with 2 ventilations being given every 15 compressions of the chest.

Poisoning

Unfortunately, there are no single signs of poisoning. Sometimes the dog will become hyperactive, sometimes severely depressed. *Any* unusual behavior may be a result of a toxic reaction, and poisoning is something to be considered. Common household items that are toxic to dogs when ingested include plants like lilies, rhododendrons, sago palms, nightshades, and Japanese yew; chemicals like antifreeze, fertilizer, rat poisons, and swimming pool treatment supplies; flea products; ant poisons; and animals such as toads, spiders, and insects. Xylitol, an artificial sweetener found in certain sugar-free chewing gums, candies, and other products can potentially cause serious and even life-threatening problems. (Such dogs may experience a sudden drop in blood sugar and become depressed, uncoordinated, or may even have seizures.) Human medications like acetaminophen (Tylenol), other pain relievers, and antidepressants can be deadly to your dog. Remember that Labradors are more likely to be poisoned than many other breeds because they will eat absolutely anything.

The effects of a toxin are not always immediate. Hours or even days can pass before you notice anything. While every toxin has

Always supervise your puppy, because his playful and curious personality could get him into trouble.

specific effects, some general signs of poisoning include:

- Inappetence
- Incoordination
- Lethargy
- Respiratory difficulties
- Seizure
- Vomiting

If you suspect poisoning has occurred, check the label on the product if possible, and read what it has to say about toxicity. The treatment will vary depending on the poison and whether it has been ingested, inhaled, or absorbed through the skin. If there's a number on the package, call to get more details. Then, call your vet or poison control center right away. Be able to provide the name of the poison; how much was absorbed, ingested, or inhaled; how long has passed since the event; how much your Lab weighs; and the signs of poisoning your pet is displaying. If your Lab is vomiting or has diarrhea, take samples to the vet to help with a diagnosis.

All poisonings should be treated as emergencies. If the exposure is to a topical poison, bathe the affected area in lukewarm running water with mild soap. If the poison is ingested, call your vet; you may be able to induce vomiting if the incident occurred less than two hours previously. (Don't induce vomiting if the dog has eaten a corrosive substance). You may also be able to give the dog some activated charcoal to delay absorption and bind the toxin.

Do not despair! The following poisons have *specific* antidotes that your vet may be able to supply right away: ethylene glycol (antifreeze), acetaminophen (Tylenol), organophosphates (insecticides), permethrins, lead, anticoagulaent rodenticides, lead, metaldehyde, snake venom, arsenic, and zinc.

If you are taking your pet to the vet, bring in a urine, vomitus, and stool sample from your dog if you can. Even if there is no specific antidote, your vet can provide supportive care like oxygen therapy, pain medication, and transfusions that may save your Lab's life.

CONVENTIONAL MEDICATION

If your vet prescribes a medication for your dog, don't leave the office without a clear understanding of what you're supposed to do with it. If there is something about the medication you don't understand, ask the vet. Here is the minimum of what you need to know about each medication your pet receives:

- What it is. You should know both the generic and trade name of the medication.
- What illness or disease it is being used to treat.
- When to give it and for how long.
- How it should be administered.
- What side effects it may have.
- How it interacts with any other medications your dog is receiving.

Dispensing Medication

Undoubtedly you will end up giving your dog medication from time to time. Doing it correctly assures that you are getting the right medication at the right time in the right dosage. The obvious first step is to follow your vet's instructions to the letter—the directions on the package may also help.

When purchasing medication, you should know that as with human medicines, some kinds are available in generic form. These are almost always cheaper and usually of the same quality as the "name brand." Although both products must meet minimum standards, sometimes the name brand does provide better ingredients. Ask your veterinarian about each specific drug.

You should not order medications and immunizations through the mail and administer them to the dog yourself, even if you know how to give shots. You may save some money, but in the long run you'll be doing your dog a disservice. This is because when you take the dog to the vet, you are doing more than getting him a shot and going home; this is a chance to speak with your vet about your concerns and observations. It's also important for the veterinarian to see your dog when he's healthy as well as when he's sick. This way, your vet can get a look at your "normal" Lab!

Ear Medication

Ear medications come in many forms: liquids, ointments, and powders. Every package has specific directions for how to

Hiding Medicine

Most Labs are enthusiastic eaters and will thrill to the anticipation of something extra tasty, like a piece of soft cheese, cooked chicken, or bread with peanut butter. All of these make wonderful things in which to hide a pill. Give a pill-less piece first, then one with the pill, and finish with another pill-less piece. Your Lab should take getting his pill in stride this way.

Herbs are often known by two or three different common names, and one common name can refer to several different herbs. To make sure you are using the one you want, go by its official Latin name, which will consist of two parts: genus and species. Mullein, for example, is officially *Verbascum thapsus*, but it still looks like mullein to me. (It makes a wonderful ear cleaner, too.)

administer that particular medication, so follow them carefully.

Eye Medication

To administer eye medication, stand behind the dog and place one hand on the side of his head to hold the head still and open the eye. Then, apply the medication with the other hand. Apply the required amount directly into the eye.

Pills

The trick to giving your dog pills is to do it so fast that the dog will be unaware he's been given a pill. In most cases, you can hide the pill in a bit of cheese, but if for some reason you can't do this, place your hand in the dog's mouth to open it and insert the pill at the base of the tongue. Once the pill is inserted, close the mouth and hold for a few seconds. You can also blow in his nose. This will force him to swallow.

ALTERNATIVE AND COMPLEMENTARY MEDICINE

Contemporary pet owners (and their vets) are no longer limited to conventional treatments. New ideas in medicine are pouring in from all around the world. Some of the "new ideas," by the way, are thousands of years old, and many are quite effective. However, you should seek the advice of your veterinarian before attempting an alternative therapy.

Acupuncture

Acupuncture was first developed by the Chinese thousands of years ago. It works by stimulating the nerves and dealing with the patient as an "energetic being." Acupuncture uses inserted needles at various body points, most of which are located at the site of major nerve bundles and blood vessels. Inserting needles seems to activate the nerves, creating a cascading effect of increased circulation and the release of healing natural chemicals. It may be used in addition to conventional medicine. Acupuncture is often used to treat arthritis pain, kidney problems, and other chronic diseases. Treatment usually takes about 20 minutes and involves the insertion of 12 to 15 needles. Benefits last about two weeks.

Acupuncture should be performed only by a licensed

The Healthy Labrador

The first step in being able to handle a sick or injured dog is to recognize some key indicators of good or failing health. If your Lab doesn't appear normal based on the following indicators, give your vet a call, describe the signs, and follow her advice.

Temperature

While taking your dog's temperature is not fun for either one of you, it's a very important indicator of many health problems. A high temperature indicates a fever, and a low one is a sign of hypothermia. Unfortunately, just putting your hand on your Labrador's nose to see if it's wet doesn't really give you a very accurate picture. (You'd have better luck testing his ears that way. Feverish dogs have hot ears, while hypothermic dogs have cold ears.)

To take your Lab's temperature, use a rectal thermometer made for dogs or a rectal thermometer made for children. In either case, coat it with petroleum jelly, insert it gently about an inch, and wait a minute so. Then, remove it and check his temperature. Normal temperature for a dog is between 100.5°F and 102.5°F.

Breathing

When your Lab is breathing normally, the chest will expand when he inhales. If the abdomen rather than the chest expands, the breathing is abnormal. Other kinds of abnormal breathing include a very slow or fast respiratory rate, loud gasping, shallow breathing, or breathing with the mouth open. The normal breathing rate for Labradors is as follows:

- puppies: 15 to 40 breaths per minute
- adults: 10 to 30 breaths per minute
- dogs who are panting from heat or exercise: up to 200 pants per minute

Heart Rate

A normal heart sound has two separate drum-like, regular beats with a silent interval between them. You can place your hand on your dog's left side while he is lying down, or you can take his pulse along the femoral artery on the inner side of his upper leg.

- puppies: 70 to 180 beats per minute
- adults: 70 to 120 beats per minute

Dogs who have been exercising will have increased heart rates.

Gums

Unhealthy-looking gums can indicate problems with circulation, breathing, infections, or even the liver. Normal gums are pink and healthy, while gums that are dark red could indicate the presence of an infection. White gums might signal anemia, yellow gums may mean liver problems are present, and dark blue gums could suggest poor circulation. If your dog has dark-pigmented gums, you can check for proper color by pulling down the skin just below the eye and examining the color of the inner eyelid.

Capillary Refill Time (CRT)

This quick test can help you check your Lab's circulation (and also tests for anemia). Press down firmly on the dog's gum and note how long it takes for the normal color to return. The CRT for a normal dog is between one and two seconds. An extremely slow CRT indicates shock or low blood pressure. An extremely rapid CRT may occur if your pet is overheated.

Hydration

Without adequate internal fluid, your dog can die. Overexertion and extensive vomiting or diarrhea can severely deplete your dog's internal water supply. To check for dehydration, collect the skin between the shoulder blades and release. Upon release, it should bounce back almost immediately. Skin that takes more than two seconds to spring back (or doesn't go back at all) is a sign of dehydration.

We are fortunate that more and more is being learned about how herbs can help prevent and cure various ailments. As with anything new or unconventional, it is best to do as much research as possible, including talking to people who have used herbal remedies, before deciding they might help your Lab. You should also consult your veterinarian.

veterinarian with at least 120 hours of study. A poorly trained person could puncture a blood vessel or do other damage.

Chiropractic Therapy

A quarter of a century ago, nobody considered chiropractic treatment for animals, but as dogs are fellow vertebrates, there's no real reason why it shouldn't be used. Benefits of chiropractic care include better circulation, mobility, and flexibility. It also reduces stress and has proven to be particularly beneficial for the canine athlete.

Herbal Medicine

Many people favor traditional methods of healing these days, and one of the most popular methods of treating disease is through the use of herbal medications. In fact, worldwide, over 4 billion people use herbs as a regular part of medical care. And while herbs can indeed heal, they should not be used except in consultation with your holistic veterinarian or a qualified animal herbalist.

Herbs are not always effective, and they are not always safe. (The same is true for modern drugs, of course.) The fact that herbs are "natural" says nothing about their safety. Rattlesnake venom is natural, too. The U.S. Food and Drug Administration classifies herbs (and vitamins and minerals) as dietary supplements—not as drugs. Therefore, herbs are not subject to the rigorous safety tests that drugs must pass before being approved. Nor do herbal manufacturing companies need to follow the same quality-control standards as drug companies. Herbs can come in many forms, and depending upon which part of the plant is used and whether it is fresh or dry, whole or extracted, tincture or tea, the strength of the medication can vary. However, progress is being made. Good herbal products carry the USP (United States Pharmacopoeia) or NF (Natural Formulary) approval, which insures that the product has been subjected to certain protocols for extracting or drying herbs. The best products also carry the stamp of approval from Consumer Lab (CL). These products have a guarantee of identity, purity, consistency, and potency.

Don't begin experimenting with herbal medications without guidance, especially if your dog is already undergoing medical treatment. Many herbs can act adversely with drugs. Don't guess. If you do decide to use herbal supplements or herbal treatment, stick with just one or two until you can understand their effects.

Herbs are the source of most modern medications, so it would be surprising if they didn't have any beneficial effects. They are most effective for chronic problems, but don't expect them to work miracles.

Homeopathy

Homeopathy is a holistic system of medicine invented by Samuel Hahnemann, a German physician and chemist, about 200 years ago. Homeopathists believe that conventional medicine is too focused on signs and symptoms of disease rather than on the patient, who, they believe, often suffers due to a physical or emotional imbalance or instability.

Homeopathy is based on the old idea of "like cures like," and in fact the name homeopathy is derived from the Greek word "homios," which means "similar." Homeopathic medicines are natural substances (derived from plants or occasionally insects) prepared by a process of serial dilution (with water and alcohol) and succession, or repeated shaking. Homeopathists believe the shaking of the substance helps to conserve its energy and potency. The final

The Lost Labrador

Losing a dog is heartrending for humans and dangerous for dogs. The best way to get a lost pet back is to make sure he has visible identification. Statistically, it has been found that most dogs with an identification tag are returned to their owners, while most who don't have one are not. Forget anything you may have heard about dogs being choked by their collars; the very slight increased risk a collar imposes is more than offset by the dangers it repels. You can also have your dog tattooed or microchipped.

If you have lost your Labrador, put up flyers with color photos of your pet all around the area in which he went missing. Put the posters at eye level, with print large enough to read from a car. List the place and date your Lab was lost, as well as his color, sex, weight, and contact information. Also, put photos at local veterinary offices and grooming shops within a one mile radius of your home. Offer a reward, but never give away all of your dog's identifying features. There are many scammers out there, so don't go alone to meet someone in a home. If possible, arrange to meet in a public place.

In addition to flyers, walk the neighborhood over and over. Knock on doors and ask if people have seen your dog. It's also a good idea to distribute your flyers to each person. Sadly, you may need to call local departments of transportation to see if any dogs matching your Lab's description have been killed on the road.

Next, go to the animal shelter in person to see if your dog is there. If you just call, the staff might just say no automatically without even bothering to check. Keep checking back every week.

Finally, call your local Labrador rescue and ask the staff to keep an eye out for your dog. Do not give up hope. I have seen dogs reunited with their owners after months have gone by!

product, which may contain extracts from more than one plant in pill or liquid form, has been diluted from ten times to millions of times.

In homeopathy, the more diluted the remedy, or medicine, the more potent it is believed to be. It seems counterintuitive that this should be so, but homeopathists swear by the results. Homeopathy does have the advantage of being inexpensive and free of side effects. It is most often used to help treat kidney and liver disease, arthritis, and hormonal imbalances.

Massage

The very touch of a loving hand is healing, and massage treatment turns a gentle form of relaxation into real therapy. Massage is an excellent treatment for older dogs, dogs with arthritis, and dogs recovering from surgery. It helps tone muscles and decrease soreness. Massage also helps reduce excess fluid around joints, stretch muscles, and increase mobility. It even helps remove metabolic waste products.

Massage may also release endorphins that ease pain. Not all conditions can be treated with massage, of course, and dogs with

Even the very touch of a loving hand can be healing for your dog.

lymphoma or fractures can be made worse with this kind of treatment. If you begin a massage program, the first session should be very short—only five or ten minutes. If your dog yawns and closes his eyes during the massage, he is probably enjoying it, and you can continue a bit longer.

SENIOR DOGS

Senior dogs often have special health needs and are more prone diseases, such as cancer, arthritis, and canine cognitive dysfunction, than are younger dogs. To help keep your senior in the best of health, it's important to establish a great relationship with your vet and make sure your senior gets a checkup at least twice a year. Your Lab's teeth are especially in need of extra attention. Keep brushing them daily, and get them professionally cleaned as often as your veterinarian recommends.

Many older dogs have built up plenty of immunity against various diseases. Talk with your vet about stopping vaccinations or reducing their frequency.

Your senior dog will have more trouble processing food than will a younger dog. Help him out by buying top quality food, with plenty of protein. (Only seniors with poor kidney function should be on a low protein food). While this is still a somewhat controversial area of nutrition, recent studies suggest that dogs in renal failure may not benefit from low protein diets and may do better on diets with at least moderate levels of high-quality protein. In fact, studies have shown that a healthy senior dog requires 50 percent more protein than a young adult! However, don't overfeed him—obesity will shorten your Lab's life.

If your senior has arthritis, it's important to support him with dietary supplements recommended by your veterinarian. And just because your dog is old and arthritic doesn't mean he doesn't need his exercise. He does, for both mental and physical reasons. He may not go fast, and it may take him a while to "warm up," but a walk two or three times a day will benefit his spirit, weight, and overall health.

Older dogs tend to chill easily, so keep him warm and comfortable and out of any drafty areas. Soft orthopedic beds are particularly appreciated.

Please continue to make your older dog a part of your life. Don't exclude him now. You owe your senior Labrador as much care now as you did when he was a playful pup.

Extra TLC
Your senior Lab needs extra love and care to help him through his golden years. Beware of potential aches and pains that didn't show before. Make sure he is eating right and getting enough exercise—and rest! You want him to be comfortable as he lives out his days.

RESOURCES

ORGANIZATIONS

American Kennel Club (AKC)
5580 Centerview Drive
Raleigh, NC 27606
Telephone: (919) 233-9767
Fax: (919) 233-3627
E-mail: info@akc.org
www.akc.org

Association of Pet Dog Trainers (APDT)
150 Executive Center Drive
Box 35
Greenville, SC 29615
Telephone: (800) PET-DOGS
Fax: (864) 331-0767
E-mail: information@apdt.com
www.apdt.com

Canadian Kennel Club (CKC)
89 Skyway Avenue, Suite 100
Etobicoke, Ontario M9W 6R4
Telephone: (416) 675-5511
Fax: (416) 675-6506
E-mail: information@ckc.ca
www.ckc.ca

Chocolate Labrador Owners Club (UK)
Secretary: Dorothy Walls
E-mail: dorothy@chocolate-labradors.org.uk
www.chocolate-labradors.org.uk

Delta Society
875 124th Ave NE, Suite 101
Bellevue, WA 98005
Telephone: (425) 226-7357
Fax: (425) 235-1076
E-mail: info@deltasociety.org
www.deltasociety.org

International Agility Link (IAL)
Global Administrator: Steve Drinkwater
E-mail: yunde@powerup.au
www.agilityclick.com/~ial

Labrador Retriever Club (UK)
Secretary: A. Ellis
E-mail: secretary@thelabrador-retrieverclub.co.uk
www.thelabradorretriever-club.co.uk

National Gundog Association (UK)
Secretary: C.B. Bexton
E-mail: chris.bexton@fsmail.net
www.gundog.org

National Labrador Retriever Club, Inc. (NLRC) (USA)
Secretary: Becky Jack
E-mail: nipntucklr@aol.com
www.labradorretrievers.org

National Shoot to Retrieve Association
226 North Mill Street #2
Plainfield, IN 46168
Telephone: (317) 839-4059
E-mail: nstrfta@ameritech.net
www.nstra.org

North American Flyball Association (NAFA)
1400 West Devon Avenue #512
Chicago, IL 60660
Telephone: (800) 318-6312
Fax: (800) 318-6318
www.flyball.org

North American Gun Dog Association (NAGDA)
13850 C.R. 31
Stratton, CO 80836
Telephone: (719) 348-5451
Fax: (719) 348-5999
E-mail: NAGDA@plains.net
www.nagdog.com

North American Hunting Retriever Association (NAHRA)
P.O. Box 5159
Fredericksburg, VA 22403
Telephone: (540) 899-7620
Fax: (540) 899-7691
E-mail: nahra@nahra.org
www.nahra.org

North American Versatile Hunting Dog Association (NAVHDA)
Box 520
Arlington Heights, IL 60006
Telephone: (847) 253-6488
Fax: (847) 255-5987
E-mail: navoffice@aol.comwww.navh-da.org

Quail Unlimited National Headquarters
P. O. Box 610
Edgefield, SC 29824-0610
Telephone: (803) 637-5731
Fax: (803) 637-0037
www.qu.org

The Kennel Club
1 Clarges Street
London
W1J 8AB
Telephone: 0870 606 6750

Fax: 0207 518 1058
www.the-kennel-club.org.uk

The Labrador Retriever Club, Inc. (USA)
Secretary: Christopher G. Wincek, Esq.
E-mail: info@thelabradorclub.com
www.thelabradorclub.com

United Kennel Club (UKC)
100 E. Kilgore Road
Kalamazoo, MI 49002-5584
Telephone: (269) 343-9020
Fax: (269) 343-7037
E-mail: pbickell@ukcdogs.com
www.ukcdogs.com
Internet Resources:

All Labs
(www.alllabs.com)
This site is a primary resource for everything one could possibly want to know about the Labrador Retriever, with links to clubs and organizations in the US, UK, and Canada, as well as showing, international rescue services, and agility training sites.

LabradorNet
(www.labradornet.com/labradors.html)
This site lists a plethora of Labrador field/hunting clubs and rescue organizations in North America and the UK. It has also compiled an extensive collection of books, periodicals, and videos on hunting, training, and health care regarding this breed.

PUBLICATIONS

BOOKS

Donner, Andrea. *What Labs Teach Us: Life's Lessons Learned from Labrador Retrievers.* Minocqua: Willow Creek Press, 2004.

Gould, Mike et al. *The Labrador Shooting Dog.* Marble: Clinetop Press, 1999.

Knutson, Paul, and Julie Knutson. *The Pointing Labrador.* Marble: Clinetop Press, 2001.

Nicholas, Anna Katherine. *Book of the Labrador Retriever.* Neptune City: T.F.H. Publications, Inc., 1990

Ziessow, Benard. *Official Book of the Labrador Retriever.* Neptune City: T.F.H. Publications, Inc., 1995.

MAGAZINES

AKC Family Dog
American Kennel Club
260 Madison Avenue
New York, NY 10016
Telephone: (800) 490-5675
E-mail: familydog@akc.org
www.akc.org/pubs/familydog

AKC Gazette
American Kennel Club
260 Madison Avenue
New York, NY 10016
Telephone: (800) 533-7323
E-mail: gazette@akc.org
www.akc.org/pubs/gazette

Dog & Kennel
Pet Publishing, Inc.
7-L Dundas Circle
Greensboro, NC 27407
Telephone: (336) 292-4272
Fax: (336) 292-4272
E-mail: info@petpublishing.com
www.dogandkennel.com

Dog Fancy
Subscription Department
P.O. Box 53264
Boulder, CO 80322-3264
Telephone: (800) 365-4421
E-mail: barkback@dogfancy.com
www.dogfancy.com

Dogs Monthly
Ascot House
High Street, Ascot,
Berkshire SL5 7JG
United Kingdom
Telephone: 0870 730 8433
Fax: 0870 730 8431
E-mail: admin@rtc-associates.freeserve.co.uk
www.corsini.co.uk/dogsmonthly

Just Labs
Editorial Offices
2779 Aero Park Drive
P.O. Box 509
Traverse City, MI 49686
Telephone: (231) 946-3712
Fax: (231) 946-9588
E-mail: kerlewein@village-press.com
www.justlabsmagazine.com

The International Labrador Review
267 Stephenson Road
Benson, NC 27504-6976
E-mail: intllabreview@aol.com
www.labradorreview.com

The Labrador International Newsletter
525 California Avenue
San Martin, CA 95046
E-mail: carpenny@labrador-siln.com
www.labradorsiln.com

ANIMAL WELFARE GROUPS AND RESCUE ORGANIZATIONS

American Humane Association (AHA)
63 Inverness Drive East
Englewood, CO 80112
Telephone: (303) 792-9900
Fax: 792-5333
www.americanhumane.org

American Society for the Prevention of Cruelty to Animals (ASPCA)
424 E. 92nd Street
New York, NY 10128-6804
Telephone: (212) 876-7700
www.aspca.org

Royal Society for the Prevention of Cruelty to Animals (RSPCA)
Telephone: 0870 3335 999
Fax: 0870 7530 284
www.rspca.org.uk

The Humane Society of the United States (HSUS)
2100 L Street, NW
Washington DC 20037
Telephone: (202) 452-1100
www.hsus.org

VETERINARY RESOURCES

Academy of Veterinary Homeopathy (AVH)
P.O. Box 9280
Wilmington, DE 19809
Telephone: (866) 652-1590
Fax: (866) 652-1590
E-mail: office@TheAVH.org
www.theavh.org

American Academy of Veterinary Acupuncture (AAVA)
100 Roscommon Drive, Suite 320 Middletown, CT 06457
Telephone: (860) 635-6300 Fax: (860) 635-6400 E-mail: office@aava.org
www.aava.org

American Animal Hospital Association (AAHA)
P.O. Box 150899
Denver, CO 80215-0899
Telephone: (303) 986-2800
Fax: (303) 986-1700
E-mail: info@aahanet.org
www.aahanet.org/index.cfm

American Holistic Veterinary Medical Association (AHVMA)
2218 Old Emmorton Road
Bel Air, MD 21015
Telephone: (410) 569-0795
Fax: (410) 569-2346
E-mail: office@ahvma.org
www.ahvma.org

American Veterinary Medical Association (AVMA)
1931 North Meacham Road – Suite 100
Schaumburg, IL 60173
Telephone: (847) 925-8070
Fax: (847) 925-1329
E-mail: avmainfo@avma.org
www.avma.org

British Veterinary Association (BVA)
7 Mansfield Street
London
W1G 9NQ
Telephone: 020 7636 6541
Fax: 020 7436 2970
E-mail: bvahq@bva.co.uk
www.bva.co.uk

DEDICATION

For my dear friend Evie Speaks, and for Alley.

ACKNOWLEDGEMENTS

Thanks to everyone at T.F.H.: Dominique DeVito, Heather Russell-Revesz, and especially to Stephanie Fornino for her kind and generous editing. A special acknowledgement to the great Labs of the world, especially the ones in my family: Birdie, Bonnie, and Duncan of Blessed Memory.

ABOUT THE AUTHOR

Diane Morgan is an assistant professor of philosophy and religion at Wilson College, Chambersburg, PA. She has authored numerous books on canine care and nutrition and has also written many dog breed books, horse books, and books on Eastern philosophy and religion. She is an avid gardener (and writes about that, too). Diane lives in Williamsport, Maryland, with several dogs, two cats, some fish, and a couple of humans.

PHOTO CREDITS

Nylabone® Cares.

Millions of dogs of all ages, breeds, and sizes have enjoyed our world-famous chew bones—but we're not just bones! Nylabone®, the leader in responsible animal care for over 50 years, devotes the same care and attention to our many other award-winning, high-quality, innovative products. Your dog will love them — and so will you!

Toys   Treats   Chews   Crates   Grooming

Available at retailers everywhere. Visit us online at www.nylabone.com